How To Strengthen Your Gut,
Lose the "But"
And Live Your
Life Regret Free

Yvonne L. Jones

Published by
Little Sepia Books Publishing
Copyright © 2018 Yvonne L. Jones
Cover Illustration Copyright © 2018
Little Sepia Books Publishing
All rights reserved.
Cover Illustrator-Richard Svensson
ISBN-10:0692401091
ISBN-13:978-0692401095

DISCLAIMER

The absence of a medical title, degree or license following my name may have already tipped you off. However, for the record, I am not a therapist of any kind. Reading this book does not create a client-therapist relationship between us. Nor should it be used as a substitute for the advice of a competent therapist admitted or authorized to practice in your jurisdiction.

Therefore, any advice, guidelines and instructions contained herein is used solely at the reader's discretion. If after reading this book and opting to apply any or all commentaries, life lessons and advice offered, the producer of this book will not be held liable if you end up with the life you've dreamed of. That part's all on you!

CONTENTS

ACKNOWLEDGMENTS

A special thanks to SWIPE Consulting for providing editorial services. Thanks Mr. Davis! Of course, there's a long list of people and things I'd like to give thanks to for sharing their insight, knowledge, wisdom, struggles and successes. Their contribution was needed to help me write this book.

However, that list of people is far too long to add here but you know who you are and I thank you all. As for the "things" I mentioned, they are all the wonderful awakenings, frustrating progressions, happy releases, unsettling realizations and exhilarating escapes.

Each of these life moments and more have helped me create a life I feel worthy of and blessed to live. I'm so thankful for it all and my thanks extends to you. Yes you, the one reading right now!

CHAPTER 1

IT'S NOT JUST IN THE JEANS

How to Strengthen Your Gut, Lose the "But" and Live Your Life Regret Free sounds more like the latest greatest workout routine doesn't it? For some it probably conjures up images of conquering one of their main goals. That being, to drop every ounce of unwanted fat from their backside while flattening and building chiseled rock-hard abs *without* regretting the process.

Who doesn't desire a fit, lean, mean, body machine that will take them anywhere they want to go in life with ease, grace, flexibility and power? You may not be there yet because you're still a work in progress, but let's just imagine how it will feel moving around in a body like that.

Do you think you'd be more confident, relaxed and at ease with yourself? Sure, you would but I think there are much better things for you to look forward to! Short of having a drop dead, stunning body or possessing a winning million-dollar lottery ticket, what can be better you ask?

Well, it doesn't matter if you are under or over weight, scrawny or flabby, young or older than young, you can still feel all of these things; confidence, ease, grace, flexibility, power, abundantly rich *and* so much more right now.

Yes, you can experience and enjoy several of the perks associated with having a fit body, and you can do so in your current not so fit birthday suit. *How to Strengthen Your Gut, Lose the "But" and Live Your Life Regret Free* has nothing to do with the size, shape and condition of your physical gut or butt for that matter.

It has everything to do with the amazing intuitive gut you are already in possession of as well as those big nagging "buts" that keep you at odds with yourself. I'll explain more about your awesome gut and those pesky buts in the coming chapters, but first things first.

I'm almost positive this goes without saying but I'm saying it anyway. It's a fact; there are no shortages of workouts and healthy regimens designed to whip you into great physical shape.

However, the problem with relying strictly on methods designed for affecting change to the outside you, are that they have no effect on the inner you, which is the place where your real issues reside. Sure, they can help you build muscle, but it won't get any easier carrying those extra pounds of regrets, doubts and worries you tend to lug around every day.

Yes, they'll show you how to burn more fat. But most fitness gurus will fail to help you melt away those everyday fears that keep expanding. Especially when you over indulge in negative conversations, draining situations and false information.

Here's my point. I'm sure you know of someone who lost a ton of weight and had gotten into great physical shape only to regain most, or all of the weight back. Then there are those who manage to keep the weight off but stress

about eating one dab too much of butter on Monday, so
they restrict their intake to only water and air on Tuesday.

Does either process or outcome seem like a happy one
to you? They were each able to lose the extra junk in the
trunk, metaphorically speaking. But can you see how not
ridding themselves of all the junk crammed inside the
interior of their vehicle, riding shot gun with them, simply
follows them around wherever they go?

Can healthy eating and physical exercise stabilize or
eradicate junk such as fears, insecurities, feelings of
unworthiness or festering doubts? Honestly, I'm not sure
which situation is worse; the one in which they regain the
weight, or the one in which they overly stress about keeping
the weight off.

At either point, neither approach seems suitable for
creating a truly satisfying existence as each seems only to
further complicate life instead of enriching it.
Unfortunately, these types of scenarios are all but expected,
even accepted in today's society. But why am I talking
about weight if weight really isn't the issue here? Well,
because size and shape ties in perfectly with the way we see
or don't see ourselves.

We have become a society overly fixated on
appearances, on how things should look great on the
outside instead of how great we should feel on the inside.
Now don't get me wrong. I am not advocating an
unhealthy lifestyle but quite the opposite. I'm more of a
champion for a person's complete health which
encompasses mind, body *and* spirit.

It's well documented. The more balanced, aligned and
complete a person feels about their inner *and* outer self,
regardless of whether others agree or disagree with their

self-assessment, they tend to experience that which they envision and desire in life. Not to mention them being virtually stress free!

Far too often we overlook the subtle components of ourselves and subsequently fail to nourish the inner being. Most often we will jump at the chance to try the latest and improved techniques designed to cut off, suck out, massage or medicate away anything that appears not quite right in our eyes.

Regardless of the cost, there's a strong desire to change what is perceived as lacking with our outer selves, and to do so as easily or as quickly as possible. There's also the need to ensure that the scrutiny of others will be positive and commendable, and that they will give their stamp of approval for our improved imagery.

Sounds like a lot of unnecessary pressure and expense, right? We have moved away from doing what makes us happy to doing what we imagine will cause others to better appreciate, more willingly accept or highly praise us for doing what we imagine they think we should be doing with our lives. Whew! I got a headache just writing that!

Because of this need to be accepted by others, many will go along with the more popular, heavily promoted idea of appearing to be something they are not. You know—fake it until you make it or fake it because you'll never make it!

However, the less commercialized, more authentic, natural desire to have the most enriching, stress-free life experiences is either considered insignificant, impossible to attain or old school.

Personally, I don't know of a single person who intentionally desires to be miserable. People want to be happy. But they have been conditioned to believe that their happiness depends on how well they fit in, or how well they can adopt the happiness standards of others.

For the person who's simply trying to fit in and be accepted by their peers, mimicry of another's idea of happiness can create an imbalance. If what they are mimicking feels contrary to what they truly believe, this conflict can't help but to result in a person yo-yoing within a few areas of their life.

The major areas we tend to yo-yo on a constant basis are relationships, finances, self-approval and decision making. Which pretty much covers any and everything. If you can name it, we can yo-yo it!

Shouldn't there come a time when one starts to question why they are choosing to live life tethered to a string? Especially if most of what's being accomplished is the back and forth swinging between barely tolerable and painful situations.

Yo-yoing is almost the equivalent of running in place during a 10-K marathon. The starter gun fires and everyone takes off, everyone except you. Oh, you're moving alright! Pumping those little arms and legs with all your might, working up a sweat *and* you're actually pointed in the right direction.

The problem is you're still in the same spot because you're running in place, and you will never make it across the finish line. Not unless they pick it up and drag it behind you. You see some misunderstand the purpose of a marathon. It's not about how good you look while you're a participant in the race. As a matter of fact, most serious running enthusiasts could care less if you're wearing high-end running gear or not.

If running is your thing, then what you and other true running enthusiasts *will* be interested in is how much ground you can cover, how much you advance while doing your personal best, and how okay you are with your own pace and the outcome.

Wouldn't it be silly to worry about maintaining the flawless look of your outfit and hairstyle as you're sweating buckets, kicking up dirt and having your do tossed every which way while you're running? The simple fact is, if your intention is to complete the race to the best of your ability, you will probably look and feel like a hot mess when you're done, and you won't care one iota!

Sometimes we get involved with activities to satisfy the demands of ego. Ego wants to be perceived in a certain way--as brilliant, talented, a team player, a leader, etc. Or maybe there's simply the expectation of receiving some type of benefit.

We may desire recognition which can lead to fame and glory, or something immediately tangible like money, a diamond ring, a gold watch or that coveted corner office with its gorgeous panoramic view!

Expecting that there be a benefit for engaging in a particular activity isn't wrong. If you have a job or a business, I'm sure you expect to earn income, to be treated appropriately and to have some leisure time off. You might even have the expectation of enjoying what you do!

What usually complicates the situation for us is when we're *not* doing whatever it is we are doing out of love, passion, genuine concern and interest. I'm pretty sure you know what I mean. Remember that thing you did for the sole purpose of rubbing it in someone's face? Yeah, *that* thing.

I'm not calling you out and you shouldn't feel like the Lone Ranger either. We've all done it! But through much aggravation and some heartache, I've learned that it rarely benefits me to engage in activities simply to prove someone wrong.

Nor was the desire to shut them up, to intentionally hurt them in some way, to cause them to feel less about themselves and envious of me, the wisest thing to do either. Whatever shallow victory I experienced by doing so was not worth the effort.

I ended up regretting it and kicking myself because my focus *could* have been directed at something fun, enjoyable, productive and more beneficial for myself and maybe others. And I can't pretend I didn't receive a warning, that quiet voice whispering in my heart to ignore my mind's ego.

"Yvonne, don't say, think or act like that. It's not worth it, just let it go."

But did I listen? No, not enough. That calm, sane voice never seemed to get any louder or more insistent than the angry, insane one I used to justify my actions. Again, you know how it goes:

*"I know they didn't! Who do they think they are? Oh no, I am **not** going out like that, like I'm some weak pushover! I didn't start this mess but I'm ending it!"*

Do you know how it feels when you remember bonehead moments in your life? Well I sure do, and I can't help but laugh at my own level of awareness and understanding at that time. After all, it was my unfounded opinion that *they* were the one's responsible for upsetting my serenity!

Was it even possible for me to get any further from the truth? Yes, it probably was, but thankfully I woke up *before* veering too far off course. I had to admit that I knew what they'd done and why they did it because *I'd* done the same thing or something similar before.

The thought of being perceived as a weak pushover came more from *my* insecurities, and not from another's pushiness. However, at the time I couldn't or wouldn't accept that reality and placed the reason or blame for the way I felt onto them. Yes, just like you I've been there and done all that too.

I know exactly how it feels to sign up for something that appears relatively simple, only to later find out that some of the facts were shrouded by my own unrecognizable fears and inaccurate beliefs. Hindsight is most definitely 20/20! However, one only gains hindsight by going through *and* learning from any challenge that needs to be faced.

Personal experience has led me to this understanding, that I can and should go through any rough patches of learning that presents itself. Taking short cuts, bypasses, placing blame or running away in the opposite direction never seems to produce the long-term advantages I desire to experience. It's seems to me that most short cuts tend to last forever and they usually end nowhere near one's desired destination.

Care to test this little theory of mine? Have you ever found yourself vexed by a particular situation in which you keep trying to avoid or get around it? But somehow, regardless of your well planned and executed maneuvers, it always manages to pop up at the most inconvenient times?

I'm certain you have because if not you wouldn't be here seeking a different mode of delivery for your desires. Wouldn't you like to stop circling around the same old undesired experiences? Instead, why not have your desires zero in on you? I'm sure you'd love that!

So, how about trying this approach instead. Stop running and wondering, and start standing and learning! Here's the best reason why you should. Learning from an unpleasant or difficult experience empowers you.

However, *not* taking the time to learn from a difficult experience only sets you up to fall for the next trap of a cleverly disguised easy appearing one. Haven't you already fallen for one too many, *"Looks too good to be true!"* easy solutions which ended up hindering or stopping you dead in your tracks?

Sure, you have. We all have but no one is stuck repeating the same mistakes. Unless for some odd reason they want to. If you opt to stand and learn, you will come to realize that all which seems difficult is not, just as all which seems easy is not. Once you grow in discernment and better recognize the subtle differences between the two, you can then use either to your advantage.

Don't you think that's great news? Being able to step *and* stay out of the yo-yo state you're currently existing in is truly a method worth learning! It's a must if you intend to change whatever is stalling your progression towards fulfillment.

So, get yourself ready and shut down any *"I can't, I don't know how to!"* self-talk. Because if I can do it so can you! It just takes a different type of inner string pulling, as well as help from available *and* reliable sources—that's all.

Yvonne L. Jones

CHAPTER 2

IF IT DOESN'T KILL YOU, YOU'RE NOT WORKING HARD ENOUGH!

I guess by now you're wondering how long it takes to whip your gut and buts into shape, and if the learning curve is easy or difficult. Well I won't sugar coat it for you. There is a slight learning curve. It can be slight, but the degree of curvature is entirely up to you.

You can make it slightly difficult or slightly easy. It all depends on how hard headed or soft hearted you are. Just a note; it goes a lot easier and quicker when you are soft headed *and* soft hearted. Throughout this book I'll try to demonstrate why this is so.

Have you ever tried to figure something out but couldn't seem to grasp an answer because it just kept slipping through your fingers? So out of habit or maybe desperation, you revert to pulling out your old but trusty manual. Perhaps you considered reconnecting with your personal guru or some newly appointed expert concerning the issue.

But somehow you just know neither will tell you anything different from what you already know. So, what's your next move? Well, you resolve to get more serious about solving this thing and begin tracking down every news article, interview, book or podcast addressing the subject.

In the process, you start to feel more like a sequestered research assistant compiling and sorting through a never-ending stream of information. All of this effort is in hopes of finding the knowledge you seek. And although you glean a bit of new insight from your info gathering, for the most part you're still empty handed.

Now I ask you, how was that even possible? Shouldn't you have found what you were seeking by now? Surely, you're not trying hard enough! What do you do next? Well, you give yourself a more motivating pep talk, (I won't even mention the language you used) change course and shift your hiney into a higher gear.

You're looking at and trying so many different methods for solving this thing until those little grey wheels spinning around inside of your head are literally smoking! At this point, it's probably safe to bet that you've invested a ton of energy into all of this activity, but you're still no closer to an answer.

To add to your frustration, you're having unsettling premonitions that if you don't slow down, streamline your focus and stop running all over the place like a chicken with its head cut off, you may have something more troubling to contend with later.

Trust me, I've seen that chicken dance before and it's *not* pleasant *or* inspiring! Let's move past headless running chickens, and onto something you can better relate to. I don't know about you, but I've never had the opportunity to witness a sane, or insane individual do what I'm about to describe next.

Just imagine a person casually getting inside of their one and only, paid for, high performance, one-of-a-kind vehicle. They then proceed to crank it up and slam their foot down on the gas pedal, holding it there until one or all of the following things happen:

1. Since they're not going anywhere, they become frustrated from sitting in one spot as they listen to their powerful, race track capable, high performance engine rev louder and louder.

2. They get light-headed and pass out from breathing in exhaust fumes.

3. The inevitable happens, the engine blows. Poof! No more functioning vehicle.

Now who in their right mind does that to something of value, to something they depend on and appreciates having? We do! *Except* not to our cars. Oh no, we wouldn't dare do that to our cherished possessions. This type of treatment is usually reserved for ourselves and sometimes others.

We will run mind, body and soul ragged. Drag ourselves kicking and screaming through or under the dirt. Then proceed to drive what's left of us to the brink of crazy with worries, fears and doubts.

It's amazing how often it fails to dawn on us to simply ease up, to take our foot off the gas pedal. That we are damaging our most precious vehicle—self, and that we're doing so in more ways than one seems to be the last thing we think of.

To say that it has taken years of painful, frustrating, exciting, mind-blowing, soul searching to get to the point where I am today is not only a mouth full, but a process I'm now grateful to have experienced.

Needless to say, all aspects of my process didn't feel good initially. Some changes were just a wee bit uncomfortable, and others were downright painful! Whether it was unpleasant or not, I was up for the challenge. I simply refused to allow a little or even great discomfort to take me out of my game!

The desire to initiate a few changes that would better assist me in life was much stronger than accepting that I couldn't remove or lessen the frustration and fear I was experiencing. I knew there had to be a way feel and experience more happiness and fulfillment in my life.

But in my zeal to correct an imbalance, I started to believe that my feelings of frustration and fear were pointless emotions to have. They seemed of no help to me whatsoever. Sounds like someone was a bit angry doesn't it? Yes. I was angry, frustrated *and* afraid. However, it eventually became apparent to me that I was wrong in my smug assumptions of those emotions being useless. Experiencing fear and frustration, even anger *did* help me.

"How so," you ask? For one, it helped me to realize that I must move past being "tired" of a chronic, disappointing situation to being **done** with it. Floundering around at the whims of my unfounded fears and frustrations, and being angry because of it was not getting me where I wanted to be.

Instead, I decided to use those experiences as a catalyst, as the best reason for change. I'm sure you've heard something similar to the following statement a million times before. Well, here comes the millionth and one time.

"Keep doing the same (unproductive, unbeneficial, hurtful) things you've always done, and you're guaranteed to continue having the same

(unproductive, unbeneficial, hurtful) results."

If you truly desire a different outcome in any area of your life, then you'll have to implement a different approach to accomplishing that desired outcome. And you can rest assured that the *better* approach will be the complete opposite of what you've been doing!

This new approach will most often require you to move outside of your comfort zone, to get *and* stay empowered, to go boldly where you've treaded lightly before, and to invest more of your focus on the things you desire to experience in life instead of the things you fear. There's just no other way to do it.

And just in case you're wondering, I am not inoculated against contracting a case of prickly fear or itchy frustration. I'm just like you. As a matter of fact, I don't believe anyone can block a particular emotion or thought, or that it's even worth trying to.

We will always have thoughts and emotions. Good, bad or indifferent, they will pop up every now and again. Sometimes they can be annoying as heck, but they can also alert us as to how we're spending our time. We can then use this information to our advantage, as a springboard for change.

One of the most important changes I made was admitting to being the only true decision maker in my life. Especially when it comes to which thoughts and emotions get to stick around. If a thought, feeling, individual or action is deemed unworthy of my focus, I simply ease into my fashionable Super Woman Teflon suit and off it slides. Oh…maybe I should clarify exactly *what* slides off. It is **not** the suit, but the attention stealer that takes a hike! Hurtful, undesired attention stealers are not allowed to get too comfortable, or to stick around and gain the upper hand.

I am highly opposed to going to bed or waking up with them, dragging their heavy "buts" around with me all day *or* playing around with them. Since they're undesired, I refuse to expend any significant amount of energy dealing with them. They are not my friends nor my enemies, *but* I'm the only one who is responsible for who or what I choose to hang out with!

Aside from the brief discomfort I went through with this learning process, I'm happy to report that I am nowhere near the place I use to be--uncertain, confused and without tangible clues of what to do next. Little did I know that what was once perceived as "winging it" or flying by the seat of my bloomers, was in fact me simply listening to and going along with a gut feeling.

Since trusting my gut more, I've learned how to better connect the dots. I know why it's important to understand my inner and outer world, and when to listen and respond appropriately. I don't always get the timing right, but I'm getting better at that too. Now, life for me feels more like riding the wave of strategically placed dominoes.

I just tip over and onto one wonderful revelation after another. There seems to be no end to these light bulb, ah-ha, gut feeling moments of mine. As a matter of fact, I no longer wonder if these moments will happen because I fully expect to have them.

Here's more good news. There are no special types or groups of individuals with a monopoly on these moments of pure insight. It doesn't just happen to the spiritually enlightened, the geniuses, the gifted and talented, the beautiful, the creative and industrious or the flat out nosy and curious ones. Yep, the last type I mentioned is most definitely me!

We all possess this ability and we each experience these ah-ha, light bulb, gut feeling moments routinely. However, most of them are blown off as mere coincidence. Like the time you decided out of the blue and at the last minute not to attend an event you had been excited about going to for weeks.

For some unknown reason you had an over whelming desire to lay across the sofa in your most comfy stay-at-home attire and catch up on a show you'd been missing. It wasn't even one of your favorite shows, but you decided to stay at home anyway.

You were about an hour into the show when breaking news interrupted your occasional nods. An unfortunate or deadly incident had occurred. It happened at about the same time you would have been on the exact stretch of road making your way to or from the event you'd canceled out on. And what was your response to this information?

"Wow, what a coincidence that happened there! Good thing I stayed at home!" said you, as if *you* had no part in protecting yourself. Like most, you believed your calm resolve to simply stay at home had nothing whatsoever to do with insight.

It wasn't like there was handwriting magically appearing on the wall, or a booming voice out of nowhere instructing you otherwise. Let's get real here. It's highly unlikely you would have stuck around and waited while that form of communiqué fully revealed itself to you anyway!

But the others, those all up in your face, don't even attempt to fix your lips to deny it ones, those out of the blue, accurate insights--we usually label correctly. Not convinced? I'll prove it to you. Do you remember that thing you were yo-yoing with, the thing that seemed bigger than life itself and capable of swallowing you whole? I will refrain from telling strangers all your business, but remember how you were scared to death of it, worried sick about it, lost sleep, friends and weight over it?

Surely you remember crying your eyes out, screaming your head off, threatening to never like, love, trust, depend on or want anything ever again. I know you haven't forgotten how you felt completely alone in your misery one moment and in the very next nanosecond, every single being on the planet was laughing at, judging or condemning you and you knew it!

Talk about throwing the best pity party known to man— you threw it! Nobody pity-partied like you did. That is, until you got fed up. By the time you'd become flat out fed up with yourself and actually got angry with the way you'd allowed things to spiral out of control, you demanded something be done about it.

You'd had it! The drama and trauma you'd gone through was more than enough and the worry, stress and pain had to stop. But the only thing you could think of to do was to prop yourself up, step into your little flip-flops, plaster a smile on your face you couldn't quite feel and vow to get through each day even if it killed you!

Then one day, seemingly out of nowhere, you had a powerful, mega-watt, light bulb, gut feeling inspired moment which jettisoned you forward in ways you couldn't have ever imagined. You received insight for the best way to deal with your "thing" issue.

Just as suddenly, almost miraculously and before you could even start to implement the insight you'd received, that troublesome thing fell neatly into perspective. It no longer had the strength of that big, bad, boogie monster you had once given it the power to wield.

Remember how you laughed with joy once you could see it as the powerless thing it truly was? It was at that point when you realized *you* were in fact the one controlling the strings all along. You were in a better position to see that you always had access to a solution.

In hind-sight, the solution was more apparent than the nose on your face! Its sheer simplicity caused you to wonder how on Earth you'd ever missed it in the first place. In that moment, you literally changed your life in the twinkling of an eye. *Now* do you remember? See, I told you!

Okay, unless you're listening to an audio, I know you can't hear or see me right now--at least I hope you can't see me, but I feel I must apologize for laughing at you. Why am I laughing? Well, because I can just imagine your little head bobbing in agreement to your very own mega-watt, ah-ha experiences.

So yes, it can feel like forever when you're in it, but the change is instant once you get it. And no, I can't even pretend it was easy while going through the hard stuff. But neither was it that difficult to change from where I was to where I intended to be.

Yes or no, easy or difficult, the choice is always, always up to us. But if you plan on being successful with this, there are a few things you will have to do, no exceptions. One is cutting some things loose, those things that no longer serve you or that never have. My personal suggestion is that you cut *yourself* some slack first.

I know. Oh, how well do I understand the desire to torpedo one's neglected or under producing garden full of withering thoughts and bug infested desires! But doing that would be overkill! You'll need to leave some remnants of your garden intact in order to implant new thoughts and desires.

Yes, there's sometime the temptation to become overzealous with snipping off those invasive worry weeds you've allowed to sprout in your freshly cultivated garden of self-awareness. But don't get too carried away with your clearing process and never over exert and stress yourself by setting time limitations.

Your process will take as long as it takes. If you remain committed to it, you will eventually progress. Actually, the more committed you are and the less concerned you are with the timing of it all, the faster your progression will be.

New insights and revelations are only realized and understood when you are open and ready for them to be. So, stop being so hard on yourself about things you couldn't have possibly known at a prior time.

Second, it is essential that you get totally honest with yourself, with why you are where you are. But you should be honest without placing blame on yourself or others. Neat trick huh? Unfortunately, because it's emotionally uncomfortable, this is the part most people will either shy away from, completely deny or minimize *their* involvement in the situation.

Sometimes…wait a minute who am I kidding here? Most times it hurts like a well-placed punch to the face when getting completely honest with yourself about yourself, and to *not* point the finger at someone while doing so. And no, I am not referring to *that* finger. You already know the index finger is the polite one to point!

Some of us (and you know who you are) hate to admit having made mistakes concerning even the smallest of things. So naturally, it seems almost sacrilegious for one to fess up to being the lone creator, facilitator and perpetrator of their own personal demons and disastrous outcomes.

Then there are some who will go so far as to state that there are absolutely no mistakes made in life ever. And to that train of thought, I can only say this:

"Really? Bull Crap!"

True, it is not a mistake that we are at certain levels of understanding and awareness in life, and that we are experiencing the consequences associated with our level of understanding.

However, most will attest to the fact that we most definitely make mistakes! But maybe the mistake-less ones are misinterpreting the word "mistake" when applied to any self-imposed, disastrous outcome. Oh wait, *that* would be a mistake and something they just don't make.

As for those of you who prefer to reside in La-La Land believing you never make mistakes, it must be quite a relief knowing you'll never have to change one single thing as it pertains to your life. Not ever!

You won't have to take up the tedious task of increasing, decreasing, walking away from or completely removing anything. Nor would it be a mistake to think you can smoke three packs of cigarettes, drink a fifth of Moonshine, eat only fast foods, snack on the equivalent of five cups of sugar every single day and *not* develop the known health issues affecting other's with similar habits.

Neither would it be a mistake to repeatedly lie, cheat on or disrespect your partner while holding onto the expectation of them never, ever getting tired of that type of treatment and dumping you!

Nope, not one of those self-centered, potential life ending actions seem like mistakes to me. You do know I'm being sarcastic, right? Making mistakes does not equate to being less than bright (smart) or to having a huge, dark, immovable boulder obscuring your path in life until the end of time.

As a matter of fact, for every mistake we can make, short of it being an immediate life-ending one, there are numerous contingencies, back-up routes in place to help move us along our chosen path.

Yes, poop does happen but more than likely you'll live to make another one! So, don't get all tripped up over making mistakes. But neither should you blatantly disregard them. Here's why.

There is no sacrificial lamb or scapegoat to suffer for, carry away or expunge you of your errors/mistakes. In fact, *you* are the sacrificial lamb *and* the scapegoat. It is totally up to you to slaughter your own fears, pride, stubbornness, blame or regrets.

If you intend to give birth to love, peace, a deeper understanding, true growth and wholeness, then it is you who is responsible for banishing what does not heal or help you. Only you can release or allow whatever binds or liberates your thoughts, feelings, desires or actions.

While it may not have been your intention or fault to have something completely undesired happen to you, you cannot deny that it most definitely was or still is your experience now.

Since it is you experiencing every bit of what happens to you, then there is no one else who can give the okay that facilitates change. Yes, the buck begins *and* stops with you! Actually, it's a good thing that all changes are up to you. Think about it.

Just imagine if any Thomasina, Dickerson or Harriett takes it upon themselves to change "correct" something about you. What if they actually had the power to do it *without* your consent, whenever and however many times they wanted to?

You'd have zero control over your life, and probably wouldn't know if you were coming or going. A puppet on a string would enjoy more freedom than you, as it has never once held a desire and subsequently lacked for anything. It has never had the ability to create, command or will anything into existence, not like you have.

Don't be fooled or frightened into believing it will be easier to just hand all your power over to someone you perceive as better in the know then you will ever be. And that by doing so you can simply sit back and play the poor, misguided, unfortunate victim in life who's waiting to be saved or let off the hook.

Forget about that. It ain't happening! And yes, that was my southern vernacular rearing its southeast-of-the-border tongue. Whereas that little trick of passing on one's power works great in the movie *Highlander,* thank goodness you don't have the ability to transfer your power in that way.

If you could it would be off with your head, end of discussion, no more of you here. Remember the chicken? Here's the only thing you can do, which is the one thing you have done consistently since you've been here. So, trust me when I say you're good at it!

The only option you will ever have is that of exercising your creative will. You will create something. It doesn't matter if you are actively focusing on a specific outcome, creating by default (unawareness) or you have given up and thrown in the towel.

Rest assured, you will reap the benefits; the outcome of either action, whether you do or not do something. So why not learn to intentionally create and do the things you truly desire as opposed to…oh let's see; helplessness, misery or hoping for the luck of the draw?

Okay, I'm off my soap box but know this. It's the things you don't know about self, the things that may not be so obvious at first glance that's hindering or even hurting you. You do realize I'm speaking from experience, right?

Once you make up your mind to rid yourself of the blocks in your life, I mean to seriously get at the root of anything that's keeping you side-tracked, it's got! And don't worry, none of your roots extend beyond the center of the Earth! Yours are nowhere near that deep.

Here's the wonderful thing about you successfully working through your very own process. You will always have a reliable method to help you uproot the things you don't want in your life, and to manifest the things that you do! You can use this process for anything you desire to experience and at any time of your choosing!

Now doesn't that sound like something you'd love to invest a small amount of energy into accomplishing? I'll just assume you said, "YES!" So, to summarize, this is not about losing physical weight. Although you should feel much lighter once you drop your buts, and much stronger as you develop your authentic gut muscles.

With this process, there are no adverse reactions to developing your gut. You can't over work or strain it. Neither do you have to worry about using any unorthodox methods, like walking backwards with your eyes crossed while chanting, *"I can see all things clearly now."*

You will learn to develop the gut strengthening method that works best for you. There is no technical jargon to figure out, so you can put away your encyclopedia or dictionary. But feel free to jot down notes or make use of a highlighter, because I will be going over some important life lessons learned. It's just us two, you and me talking about life in general, love, happiness and some of the other stuff in between. I'll be sharing with you some of the simple techniques I have discovered.

These are easy techniques to implement. They can help you to eliminate a lot of the stress and fear incorrectly associated with the way life is in general. Life does not have to be something that dictates over you or beats you down! It can be much more enjoyable if you're not guessing at it, struggling against it, dodging punches or worse, giving up!

More importantly, you will come to know that there is no "secret" nor has there ever been one concerning manifesting or living the life you desire. This knowledge has been available since man has been able to communicate the awareness of it. It's neither a secret or new. However, just like anything else in life worth accomplishing, it does take a degree of discipline and awareness if you want to be consistently successful at it.

The fact that you are reading or listening to these words right now means that at some point in your life you were disciplined and aware enough to learn how to read, *and* most likely to write. I said, *"most likely to write"* because *my* handwriting is atrocious, but I can't speak about yours! Some will execute their enunciation and penmanship skills flawlessly and some will not.

Nevertheless, at some point and through consistent application, each can be understood, to get their point across *and* to get what they want. Regardless of one's technique or style, that's all manifesting is and it's what we do 24/7. We just don't call it manifesting, we call it *Living!* Finally, it shouldn't take you any longer to get a grasp of things than the length of time it will take you to read this very short, uncomplicated book.

If you're tired of all the black eyes and bruises you feel life is raining down on you, then let's move closer to a remedy, shall we? It's got to be better than what you're doing now—listening to and sitting on all your buts!

CHAPTER 3

THE ANATOMY OF A BUT

I bet you had no idea you'd be in school today, *but* we're always in school. We each attend the highest acclaimed educational institution in the entire universe. I know you've taken at least a few classes at the School of Life before, right?

Since you're a returning student with a few terms already completed, think of this as a refresher course. You can attend at your leisure, and there are no tests or exams to cram for. As a matter of fact, these will be open book sessions only. *But* as your instructor, my only requirement is that you open up and allow that inner teacher to enlighten you further. Let's begin!

What is the definition of the word but? Most of us learned this in grade school, and as you probably remember "but" is a conjunction, a preposition and an adverb. I will use an example of each instance.

Conjunction: *"The concept has worked for others, but I didn't think it would work for me."*

Preposition: *"No one was of help **but** me."*

Adverb: *"I am **but** a temporary employee."*

Do you see how the versatile "but" connects opposing thoughts, makes exceptions to the rule and places higher or lower value on words, thoughts and feelings?

*"Man, if I had a dollar for every time I used the word but in a negative, self-defeating, victimizing way I'd be rich, **but** I'd probably blow the money."* See what I mean?

How many times has someone (or self) spoken success into your life only to have you shoot it down with a but? Allow me to remind you if your memory is a bit foggy. A friend who knows you extremely well says to you the following:

"I think you'd do great at that job! You're already doing something similar." However, the less aware *you* who doesn't have faith in the things you are capable of doing, responds in this way:

*"**But** I don't think I know enough, I'm not qualified. They'd never hire me anyway."*

Do you see what you did? You took that strong, positive, heart-felt, more than likely accurate assessment of your true abilities and ripped them to shreds. You hobbled your success with your very own negative, unsubstantiated thoughts and words.

More than likely you feared you were not capable of successfully fulfilling the expectations that position held. In your mind you believed you were not qualified. Because you felt unqualified, you reaffirmed that belief by speaking it into existence.

You were probably already thinking and feeling a bit insecure about your abilities in certain areas. But now in this particular area, you've announced your intentions to be completely unqualified to yourself and the entire universe!

What could have been a fleeting worry or doubt, something easily correctable with more training or self-empowerment, instead you opted to infuse these perceived limitations with more staying power.

I'm not beating up on you, we all do this. Usually, we're our own worst critic and bully. And the unsettling thing is, it's seldom realized by us that we were doing such undermining things to ourselves. I said *"were doing"* because all that's about to change, right? Right!

Sidebar: I think there's a reason every major religion, pragmatism's practical yet logical stance, and one's everyday dime store version of common sensism (that's a new term I just made up) hits on this very simple yet comprehensive principle. The Golden Rule. Treat one another, which by the way includes self, the way you intend to be treated; loved, cared for, appreciated, talked to, etc.

In its simplicity, The Golden Rule covers quite a few things if you care to take the time to delve deeper into this area of thought. I've paraphrased the Golden Rule, not for any religious implications it may have, but for its ability to provide simple, clear and concise guidelines for beneficial decision-making and conduct.

Obviously, I have no idea which religious dogma—if any, you adhere to. But it doesn't really matter. When you can shoot yourself in the back with your own thoughts and words, then where will your help come from? When or however it comes, you will do what you've become accustomed to doing; kill the bearer of great news and of your most desired gifts and blessings. Stop doing that!

Does it sound like I'm admonishing you right now? You're correct, I am! But I'm doing so with love and compassion. I'm trying my very best to shine a light on some things you may not be aware of. At least not on a consistent enough basis, or else you wouldn't be here with me now. You're either extremely bored, or seeking answers as to why you haven't accomplished or progressed more in certain areas of your life.

The forever optimist in me is betting on you being the seeker. Likewise, my initiative side is almost positive you have a "gut feeling" it's not something outside of yourself that's doing all of the hindering and keeping you hostage, trapped in a place you'd prefer not to be.

Often it is those glimpses of truth about ourselves that we try to run from the most. Yes, we try but we also know it's impossible to out-run ourselves. Let's get back to that gut feeling I just mentioned, because it is the part of you that must be fully activated and developed.

The sooner you begin using and relying more on your intuitive gut, the sooner you will stop second guessing your decisions, sabotaging your efforts and fearing the known and unknown. You'll become better equipped to stop all the incessant running around and worrying that your sky is falling.

Instead, you will learn to shift more of your energy and focus into creating, experiencing and loving the life you have right now. This also includes manifesting those experiences you desire to have at some future point in your life! The clarity and empowerment you'll gain from your unique process will be priceless, and you will come to know yourself so much better.

Nothing will be able to rattle or shake your foundation, at least not for very long. As soon as you become aware of any misalignment, you'll know how to immediately ease right back into an aligned state of being. The only difficult part if any, is to stay aware of how you're feeling and thinking. Now let's talk more about how a gut feeling comes about and what it actually does for you.

In opposition to popular belief, a gut feeling does not spring from one's imagination or fears, and it most definitely isn't privy to any accurate or inaccurate beliefs one holds claim to. Nor is it brought about by the habits and routines we often incorporate into our daily lives.

A gut feeling comes about because at some point we've asked a question or made a statement about something we'd love to experience or better understand. The question or statement can be thought, or spoken out loud. Most don't realize they have even asked a question, because sometimes it feels we're simply acknowledging something we haven't before—that we are just curious about it.

At the time, the question may have been considered by us to be trivial, or of the utmost importance. And sometimes these questions will linger in our mind for days, while at other times they will be forgotten almost as soon as they are thought of or spoken. But it seems that merely in the asking or curiosity and feeling of a thing, we activate a response.

Usually as a precursor to an answer, one begins having moments of synchronicities related to the thing they desire to better understand or experience. Let's say you may hear a street musician playing a flute and it instantly brings back pleasant memories of your days in high school band.

You were a good clarinet player back then, but that wasn't your first instrument of choice. The flute was what you really wanted to play. Now, the sound of your first choice stirs something in your soul. It is so lovely and soothing that it causes you to briefly wonder if you could ever learn to play a flute in that way.

31

Before long, you're hearing flute compositions everywhere! Be it in a jazz instrumental on the radio, a movie score or a commercial. You suddenly realize that even your favorite personal music collections have brief but haunting sessions of a flutists in them.

Eventually you listen to all that your gut feeling has been showing and telling you, that learning to play a soul stirring flute is something you can and should do! That was your initial intention years ago but somehow you talked yourself out of it.

Whether we are being naysayers, responding from a state of supreme fear and panic or calm serenity, a response always follows a question. But we may not clearly hear or understand it if we've worked ourselves into some frantic or numbed state of being.

In my opinion, when understood and taken heed of, a gut feeling is the best answer or instructions one can receive. Since these replies appear to be uniquely tailored to the individual, it is also my impression that these gut feeling answers come from an infinite, universal, collective consciousness.

I envision it as a cumulative, creative stream of love, knowledge and wisdom in which we can all tap into *and* contribute to at any given moment, whether we realize it or not. You may call this loving stream of infinite knowledge, creativity, power and awareness whatever you like. I have no desire to agree or disagree with the name chosen. It is what it is to you.

But hopefully you will be more interested in knowing that there is no trick to strengthening your intuitive gut. Whether you've ever given it enough thought or even acknowledged it, you *have* and will continue to use it in some capacity.

However, it may astound you to learn that most would rather develop their buts instead of their gut, since they have been doing it that way for quite some time. Oh, but you probably already know that part.

Do you ever wonder why we are so unaware of what we are doing, or not doing when it comes to making the best decisions and choices in life? I think it's all about one's perception. I'll explain what I mean by using this one perception many of us have.

Most of us view past or present life events as real, and future events as likely to occur. And whereas past events may have actually occurred, I say *"may have actually occurred"* because sometimes we get the details wrong about them. Wait a minute...come to think of it, sometimes we get the details wrong about present events as well!

Unlike one's past or present reality, future events have yet to fully materialize. They have partially materialized because of our desire for that future event happening. It *is* presently thought, sensed within us and acknowledged. In other words, it seems very possible and real to us, regardless of the fact that we cannot physically see, feel, taste, touch or smell it yet.

But it can feel as if it will or will not happen because we have an astounding ability to fixate on stuff! In most cases fixating isn't an unproductive thing to do. What makes it a good or bad experience simply depends on what and how we fixate/focus.

The results, the outcomes we experience in life is always in line with one's focus and feelings. Is one's fixation on a thing that's desired or not desired? Does one feel confident that it will somehow come about, or do they feel certain of it never coming to fruition?

Usually, these imagined future events we desire to experience (or not to experience) elicit such intense focus *and* feelings that like a fish on a hook, we pull them into the now. Now is our present and continuous state of being. However, we can and often do pull past and perceived future events into the present moment.

I can just imagine you're looking sideways at this page right now! So, I'll give you a moment to think about the ways we merge past, present and future experiences. Then I'll give you my take on that neat little trick we all do so well! Are you done? Okay, here I go.

Our thoughts and feelings eventually manifest into something tangible, real. Again, manifesting is not some "New Age" process recently discovered. We've *always* done it! As we think so we are. But unlike a coin flipped in a game of chance, we need only to add focus and feeling to the thought of a desire and we're guaranteed to produce one of the following results. Never is the outcome the result of chance.

One Outcome: Because you remained focused on experiencing exactly what your desired, the coin had no other option but to land face-up and grant you that desire.

The Other Outcome: Because you fear-focused on experiencing the exact opposite of the thing you desired, the coin had no other option but to land tails-up and grant you that undesired thing.

Allow me to explain a bit more about how we manifest what we do not desire to experience. It will be a true eye opener! Let's stick with the coin analogy. The position that flipped coin lands on depends on two things, one being *how* we fixate/focus. For instance, the intensity level. How often, long or short, dreadful or happy is our point of focus, and how intense or not is the emotional feeling we've attached to an object of focus.

Obviously, the other component is *what* we fixate/focus on, be it an event or situation, a person, an object or even a feeling. Both what and how we fixate is essential to what will manifest in our lives and how fast or long it will take that manifestation to occur.

Let's say I'm deeply committed and focused on becoming a doctor. From the very start, it's understood that certain skill sets will have to be acquired, and that it will take years of studying, internships, money and a few other things I may not have considered.

But because I'm more dedicated to focusing on successfully completing each and every step (either known or unknown, easy or not) then accomplishing the goal is what is drawn into my reality. In time, I will move from a pre-med student to a full-fledged doctor. Which is what I set out to do and to be.

It works the same if my focus is more on the things I fear will stop, or greatly hinder me from becoming a doctor. What if I begin focusing more on unfortunate and painful things that happened to me in the past, or the awful things that *could* happen to me in the future?

I can become consumed with the memory of a time in my past when there was not enough time, money, skill set, or the acquired knowledge needed to complete a project I desperately desire to realize. Because this has happened a few times in my past, more than likely I will begin envisioning my future to be racked with the same setbacks.

If I consistently continue to focus in this manner, then there's no way I'll become a doctor! What I will manifest instead are situations in which I will **not** have enough time, money, acquired skill set or adequate knowledge to accomplish that which I desire to experience. In fact, I will have set in motion the actualization of a uniquely tailored, self-fulfilled prophecy of failure! My dreaded past and aptly perceived future will find its home--be manifest within my present time.

As you can see, it doesn't matter if what I focus on is perceived as good or bad for me, desired or not desired by me. What and how I focus on a desired *or* undesired thing is what and how I will experience it. Just know that every present moment includes past memories and future expectations.

Think about it. We do nothing outside of the now and if you come to understand this then it will behoove you to focus your thinking and feeling on those things you will love to experience and not focus on the things you fear experiences.

I hope you will latch onto this concept, that it's how and what we think and feel that works for or against us. No one's life is determined by the whelms of chance, academia, social status or wealth. Awareness and focus are the force that dictates which realities we live to experience.

My advice is to choose wisely and with the best of intentions, because what you experience will either be the reality you choose to love and accept, or the reality you choose to fear and regret. Sounds pretty cut and dry doesn't it? So why did it take me *forever* to get this?

I'll explain why in just a bit but for now, let's get back to that coin because in a worst-case scenario, some will become trapped in indecision, doubt and fear. They will keep their coin in a continuous spin cycle, flip-flopping between love, abundance and possibilities to fear, lack and improbabilities.

There have been many greats teachers to speak about

this acrobatic form of indecision and doubt. The Buddha has been quoted as saying:

"There is nothing more dreadful than the habit of doubt. Doubt separates people. It is a poison that disintegrates friendships and breaks up pleasant relations. It is a thorn that irritates and hurts, it is a sword that kills. Neither naked asceticism, matted hair, dirt, fasting, sleeping on the ground, dust and mud, nor prolonged sitting on one's heels can purify a man who is not free of doubts."

The Bible references this type of activity as well.

"A double minded man is unstable in all his ways."

Prolonged indecision and doubt can result in one being lukewarm, neither hot/passionate nor cold/dispassionate, but virtually existing within a self-imposed stalemate. Chronic doubt demonstrates a lack of conviction and nullifies whatever is desired or hoped for. It's a mind-set that should be avoided because remaining in a state of doubt or indecision, sitting on the fence and mentally flip-flopping never advances anyone!

Or look at it this way. Can you imagine going to your favorite restaurant, ordering a tall glass of cold, sweet tea, taking one deep sip and immediately realizing it's too hot, too tart *and* salty, but never admitting how bad it tastes?

Will you (with the help of functioning taste buds) debate with yourself as to whether or not you'll continue consuming that nasty concoction? How long will it take you to inform the server how disgusting their "sweet tea" really is before demanding a replacement, or asking for your money back?

I'll answer those for you. *"No, not very long and I want a refund right now!"* I'm not one-hundred percent sure, but I'm betting on you responding fairly quickly to a foul taste in your mouth. As for me, it would be a knee-jerk response.

My taste buds would revolt at about the exact moment my brain is broadcasting a red alert. **Spit It Out Now!**

Not hesitating when you know or sense something is not beneficial for you, can be helpful in avoiding a few adverse side effects. In this case, an upset stomach, food poisoning or worse, death by contaminated tea!

Even a baby, who has yet to develop the most discriminating taste buds, would be slow or indecisive about responding to a foul taste in their mouth. Babies have no additional concerns connected with reporting what does not please them.

Baby could care less if someone's watching them express their displeasure, if the cook or server will be docked, or whether or not the health department rains down on the establishment. In rapid response to encountering such nastiness, baby will immediately distort that once beautiful face, spit out the offensive substance, release a full body tremor, and then proceed to scream in high acoustic stereo surround sound!

Not only will baby clearly and unashamedly demonstrate a dislike for the establishment's sweet tea, everyone else in the room will see it as suspect too. Yet, how often do we grown folks lose ourselves within the unproductive realm of self-debate? Especially when it's concerning an issue we know is not pleasing to us!

If something is not pleasing to you, why defend it, why continue to uphold it? I think by now you have a better sense of how detrimental it can be just sitting on your "buts" spinning. Ouch! I just pictured that. Not only does it sound painful, it looks painful and that's because it *is* painful.

It's painful not being able to move in the direction you want, or to not catch hold of the things you desire. It hurts feeling left behind and being in total despair because you're so confused, fearful or plum tuckered out until you don't know what to do next.

When you find yourself at this point, the high-pain point, don't you give up! There is a way to use it to your advantage. Yes, you read correctly. You can and should use a but pain to your advantage. It's not like you haven't done it before, turned a painful but situation into a beneficial one.

However, I completely understand that dealing with painful encounters can cause you to be a bit apprehensive. Still, there's no better time for you to take a stand, for you to get off your "buts" so you can move on from there. Come on now…bust a move!

Yvonne L. Jones

CHAPTER 4

COIN TOSSING,
FENCE SPINNING AND OTHER
SURREAL LIFE WORKOUTS

Remember that coin we spent in the last chapter? How about we bring it to life? Let's pretend that each individual is endowed with a magical coin. On one side is everything the owner of this magical coin could possibly desire and more.

Can you guess what's on the opposite side? Well, that side of the coin may contain things the owner does not desire which may or may not be a bad thing. It all depends on whether or not one is coming from awareness or unawareness.

Most of us are usually not aware of what's all available to us. We have been instructed or taught ourselves to place some experiences out of reach. They are perceived to be off limits for a number a reason—most of which are invalid. Let's up the ante and picture the opposite side of the coin as a queue, a holding pen for flashes of thoughts and ideas that haven't quite made it to that strong, desired stage yet. They're possible to attain, but there's no certainty of experiencing them for now.

Initially, we have no idea which side of our coin generates what. We are simply given our very own unique and magical coin, instructed to use it wisely and promised that help will always be available. In essence, we'll have to figure out how to work this coin through use, but assistance when needed is provided.

During the process of learning how to fully activate this magical coin, some start to pay very close attention to the possibilities both sides of their coin has to offer. Eventually some come to realize the coin can be positioned according to a desired outcome.

They can simply keep it on the side that most often grants or facilitates their desires. By becoming more aware of the results from previous tosses or flips of their coin, they no longer have to wonder or guess if there is a chance of it landing on the side they prefer. No more games of random chance for these folks!

Then there are the others. These are the ones who will toss their coin without giving it a second thought. They become mesmerized as their shiny, golden coin rises high in the sky and glimmers as it catches the light in rotation. It's such a beautiful sight to see that in their zeal to toss their coin again, they fail to take note of which side it lands on.

This failure to take note happens over and over again, as does the failure to acquire their desires. Of course, occasionally it appears they get "lucky" and land a desire here and there. But they never know how it comes about. Unfortunately, they continue to ignore which side of the coin generates a thing desired or intended as opposed to a thing not desired or feared.

Life is just like that magical, golden coin. We are each given a life with beautiful and powerful magic and whether one cares to admit it or not, we are instructed to use it wisely.

Life instructions come from a number of sources, from one's inner being, from parents, other care givers, family members and friends, teachers of every discipline and yes, even strangers. However, it is completely up to the bearer of this coin of life to grow in knowledge *and* wisdom, because no one can give you those. At least, not without your participation.

Whereas knowledge is the learning and then the application of certain techniques, wisdom is much broader and encompasses far more than knowledge alone. Wisdom comes from truly engaging in life, and not hiding, running away or denying those life experiences. It comes from paying attention to the outcomes created by your and others actions. I'm sure you've heard the following terms before:

"Wise as Solomon." Or "Smart as a whip, but not one ounce of common sense!"

With wisdom we are much better able to make the necessary corrections or adjustments as we become aware of the need to do so. And as you may have already guessed, that help along the way we were promised to have is none other than the creative, intelligent force which seems to initiate and animate all things.

More important for us, this force seems to inhabit the seat of the soul, and comes to us by way of our intuitive gut, the spiritual umbilical cord which connects us to this Source Force of life. It is that inner, deep-core feeling we pay attention to on occasion.

But it's your life and no matter what anybody says about

your life condition, you have the power to do with it what you will. You can toss it around willy-nelly and never take note of where, when or how you land. You can pimp it out if it gets a little dull and faded, and even lend it out if you are just that bored, lazy, scared or unsure of what to do with it next.

Or if all else fails, you can do absolutely nothing productive with it at all. Remember that fence spinning fiasco? We have in this life the ability to do a lot of wonderful and exalted deeds, or horrible and lowly ones. We can call forth our most ardent desires, or our worse fears by simply thinking and speaking them into existence.

But just as easily, we can change our thoughts or talk and release a desired or undesired thing. This is why it is imperative we grow in wisdom and learn to better utilize our gut feelings. Because doing so enables us to by-pass a boat load of hurt!

Most of us possess first-hand knowledge of how difficult it is to avoid some pains in life. It can be difficult because prior to these pains coming about, we didn't expect or foresee them happening. We don't know what there is to know until we know it!

For example, we don't usually foresee uninvited guests, having our first impacted wisdom tooth, being stuck in new road construction or a sudden traffic accident in which no one in the vicinity gets to avoid.

Even though we cannot know most things before hand, we *can* analyze the origin of a pleasant or pain producing occurrence. Then we can envision there being an advantage of either outcome, whether it's pleasant or painful.

If uninvited guests are a pain because your house is always a hot mess and *not* that the guests themselves are unwanted, then that's a little hint for you to get yourself in order. Nine times out of ten, if your house looks and feels like the kick-off to World War Y, then other important things are more than likely disorganized and scattered as well. Like your thoughts, daily routines and projects.

However, if your guests *are* contributing to your pain, then you will have to address that with them and resolve the issue to your satisfaction. Remember, it's your life and fortunately you get to decide how you live it, and who you intimately share it with! If your guest is not willing to get on board with your unique life desires and experiences, then allow them to get on board with someone else's. Preferably their own!

Oh boy, wisdom tooth pain. Now this one is a doozy! Yes, it can be extremely excruciating, but is the easiest to resolve as it is a localized pain in the body. It doesn't take root (pun intended) because of a habit, belief or patterns of thought. However, if you have any unresolved fears of dentists, then wisdom tooth pain will be extremely helpful in releasing those fears.

"How," you ask? Here's how.

Once that impacted tooth begins throbbing none-stop, up and down the side of your head and neck, you will *run* to a dentist office and beg either the dentist, their assistant, the front office help or the janitor to remove it by any means necessary! Afterwards you will love any and all dentists. Guaranteed!

What can I tell you about driving or creeping in traffic, that it sucks? Yes, it does but sometimes it's avoidable by either starting out on your destination earlier or later. You can also opt to ride your bike and take the back streets, or car pool, take the bus or train and leave the driving and frustration to someone else.

Here's a thought. If all else fails, you can gracefully except the fact that there are some things in life you cannot change or get around. However, it doesn't mean you can't change the way you feel or how you respond to any unchangeable facts of life.

If you are to avoid chronic high blood pressure, tension headaches, dangerous road rage incidents or incarceration, you will have to find a way to deescalate the feeling of having no control over the situation.

The response to this pain is in letting go of one's perceived control over things outside of themselves. We cannot control when or where road construction begins or ends. And that extremely slow, reckless or clueless driver, we can't control them anymore than most of us can control the weather.

With the unpredictable and often unavoidable occurrence of traffic, the one thing in our control is how we handle the situation. Do we curse everyone or thing we feel is responsible for holding us in grid-lock? Or do we chill out and spend that time more productively by listening to an instructional CD, or a comforting music track?

You see the purpose of pain or discomfort is not to make your life a living nightmare. On the contrary, it is designed to draw attention to the parts of you that are either being ignored, overly stressed, under developed, underutilized, or that needs to be removed completely!

Pain is a gauge, an alarm *and* self-diagnostic tool all in one. But in order to benefit from this magnificent multi-functioning bio tool, we have to become more attentive as to how we're feeling, and to what we're thinking or saying. Most definitely, we need to abandon the practice of blaming something or someone else for the pain we're experiencing. Okay, we're done here, but allow me to digress just a bit.

Do you remember us discussing that immaculate, charming place you love inviting certain guests to on occasion? Yes, that place. How about we mosey on over there? You do know how to get there from here, don't you? It is the place you call home. So, go ahead, slip on your ruby running shoes and let's head there now!

Yvonne L. Jones

CHAPTER 5

IF THERE'S NO PLACE LIKE HOME, WHY ARE YOU ALWAYS AT THE GYM?

What is home to you? Is it a place where you have experienced your happiest moments, and where your most cherished memories reside? Is home any place where moments of happiness and contentment seem to swallow you up completely? Does it matter how often or fleeting the memory of home may be because the thought of it always leaves you with such a warm, fuzzy feeling?

Is there a certain scent, feel or look that reminds you of home? Is home linked to a specific time in your life? Or do you simply carry the idea of home around with you, no matter the season, no matter the reason? I'm pretty sure you answered an astounding *"Yes!"* to at least one or more of my questions.

So, it's unanimous! You are at home one-hundred percent of the time. Who'd have thought it? Oh, wait! Did you think home was a structure you'd have to find your way back to in order to experience it again? Is that why you're at the gym so much, because you can't imagine or feel your way back home?

I'm using the following phrases, the Gym, gym mentality and gym rat as metaphors for the mental places we go to, and the activities we over indulge in whenever we feel unsure or insecure.

Usually we find ourselves lurking within the dank, dingy recesses of the Gym whenever we start believing others light shines brighter than our own. It is the go-to place for up and coming gym rats seeking to prove themselves worthy, capable or better than others.

If one is properly outfitted and looks to be performing the appropriate moves, then they are elevated by their peers to gym rats with rank! Rank meaning a particular status level and not necessarily stinky.

Fortunately, the type of gym I'm referring to is not for everyone. Some will fail to develop the strong gym mentality needed to survive in such a harsh environment. Instead of becoming dedicated gym rats to the core, they will either become disempowered followers, uninspired spectators or eventually gym rat dropouts.

For new gym rats, repeated visits to the Gym cultivates the illusion of progress. Newbie's are instructed by Master gym rats to at any cost, go beyond their perceived limitations.

"Push harder until it hurts! No pain, no gain! Work until you drop! There's no time for thinking about how you feel! Just do what I do and you won't even recognize pain anymore!"

These wide-eyed, devoted gym rats are convinced that since the Gym Masters already possess the things they themselves desire to be or to have, then they will hang on every word or set of instructions given to them—literally!

Somehow, they manage to stay receptive to this type of gym mentality for a while. But try as they might, it's hard to ignore just how painful and defeating it can feel to be a member of the Gym. For many, getting lost through repetitive rounds of unproductive, emotionally numbing mental and physical work outs, never seems to bring about the changes they envision.

Some simply can't get past the unsettling notion of incorporating concepts or ideologies that are contrary to their core beliefs and desires. This in turn makes them question their reasons for enduring the physical discomfort of activities designed to embed undesired concepts.

Eventually, they lose all of their enthusiasm and joy in the process. Once they break away from the illusion of the Gym, they can't help but to ask themselves the most obvious question of them all.

"Why the heck was I even there?"

When you think about it, these things happen at a brick and mortar gym as well. There's really no wondering why quite a few stops attending and cancel their membership all together.

In spite of the additional mental and physical effort required, as well as the monetary expense and time spent at the Gym, the best desired changes were seldom realized or sustained. Their "buts" were as big as ever *or* bigger, and their gut was still weak from workouts not tailored for strengthening their unique structure, condition or level of receptivity.

Dropping one's gym mentality and working out at home (although working *in* is a better analogy) should allow some to better understand why their heart just wasn't in the gym scene in the first place. The Gym really isn't the ideal place for a sensitive, empathetic heart. All that's required at this particular type of Gym is as much energy, sweat and tears as one can spill!

If you've watched the movie *The Karate Kid*, you may understand the point I'm trying to make concerning the Gym, gym mentality and gym rats. However, if you for whatever reason have missed this wonderful enlightening movie, here's a very quick overview:

Sweet, lovable, scrawny lad desires to fit in and not be bullied anymore. He decides to join a certain gym with other gym rats while under the tutelage of a powerful and knowledgeable (technique wise) master karate gym rat.

But he soon learns that this particular master karate gym rat and his gym rat disciples are full of themselves, mostly dishonorable and uncaring of anyone deemed "weak" and not up to their level of physical power or deviant mental stealth.

They are without a doubt under the spell and illusion of their unhealthy brand of gym mentality. Eventually, tensions rise and Scrawny lad no longer desires to be associated with, let alone trained by such a knowledgeable scum bucket. He's disappointed but fed up, so he drops his gym membership.

But just when scrawny lad thinks he will be scrawny forever, he is provided the perfect teacher. In time, what scrawny lad learns from his Source-Force provided, spiritually aware, kick but(t) teacher is that his inner and outer power comes from his inner strength *and* outer gentleness.

He begins to understand that true mastery comes from self-awareness, self-empowerment *and* genuine love and concern for self and others. The End. But not really, as this story is forever evolving. Okay, let's tidy this up and bring it on home!

I'm sure you've heard the saying, *"Home is where the heart is."* What does the word heart mean to you when used in this context? Is it the love you feel, the very core or essence of your being, or the beating organ inside your chest? Most will agree that it is all three and so do I, but it is so much more than that. Hang with me, I'm going somewhere with this train of thought.

If home is where the heart is, and the heart represents the core of love itself, the place where one's deepest affections reside, then it stands to reason that *you* are always at home. I know you think it's not that simple, but stick with me for a minute more.

Where does love come from if not from or through the individual? Love is not something you can pick up at a special place, as if it can be packaged and then handed out like a to-go meal.

It's not something that can be acquired from outside of one's self. One can only express/show, and experience/feel love. It cannot be given *or* taken away because the intended recipient can only experience what *they* perceive is another's expression of love.

Because feeling love (or any emotion) is a heart-mind state of being, a feeling we each experience and interpret in our own unique way, the process almost seems to take the other party out of the loop doesn't it? Isn't it a wonderful thing that we came here with love already hard-wired, already installed and that no one can hand it to us or take it away?

Try as you might, not even you can do that. From the sociopath to the saint, we each express and share a love for something. Love is the most advantageous emotion expressed and experienced by mankind, be it parental, spousal, friend, pet, creative expression, talents or the love of nature.

With all of love's various degrees of intensities, sentiments, understanding, history and desires packed inside of it, no one is left wanting! Oh, you can lose sight of it, suppress or even distort it by forgetting or never really knowing who or what you truly are. But you will never be rid of it.

From every angle you use to explore the location of home/love it somehow comes right back to you, as you are always there, because *you* are the living embodiment of home/love itself. Wherever you go, there you are and there love is too!

No matter where your head (intention or state of awareness) and feet (path or course of action) takes you, you're still at home! Home being the inner you, and not some outer structure, concept or venue.

You are the most perfect, fully sustainable and portable home that there is, except most don't believe this is even possible. However, your inability to believe that you and home/love are synonymous is not all your fault. We each have had plenty of help in the *"find home/love outside of yourself"* arena.

There are more levels to us than we are aware of, and most are just beginning to scratch the surface of their current level. But scratch...no *rise* above it, we can! If we don't, how else will we fully come to know and activate the loving, wonderful, creative, powerful beings hidden beneath all those layers?

Yes, I understand it's a bit scary realizing just how magnificent and powerful you truly are, and that the course of your life path is left up to you. But I believe, and hopefully you will also come to this realization--that having this awareness and ability beats the alternative.

That being, you waking up one morning to find your wonderful home/love buried beneath a landslide of standardized beliefs, antiquated custom's and incomplete or compromised teachings.

As a result to this undesired form of burial, we can become fearful, unhappy and indecisive in our own home. Not to mention becoming overwhelmed by all the digging we'll have to do to free ourselves!

We are not imperial mummies to be preserved beneath the dirt and held in reverence for generations to come. We are unique and special living beings meant to experience, contribute and co-create with others while building upon this stuff we call life!

This can only be accomplished while standing *on* the ground we cultivate and build upon. Hopefully, we will do these things *for* the benefit of self, for current as well as future generations, and not for any reverence we may deem ourselves worthy of receiving.

There's really no mistaking this, that each of us is meant to be the ruler of our own abode. We are not meant to only be the grounds or housekeepers. Yes, those duties are important ones, but they become pointless without a capable ruler in the house.

You can keep the house clean and the grass cut, but if you fail to repair a substantial growing crack in the foundation, then what's the point? That spotless house with its beautiful manicured grounds will eventually fall in on itself!

Every successful and even a mediocre ruler has learned how to rule their domain. Those who rise above the rest do their homework first by educating or familiarizing themselves concerning any subject of interest or desire. However, their educational process does not consist of the endless gathering of facts and stats.

They get just enough knowledge and then act upon what they know while tapping into their intuitive gut. By aligning themselves with their intuitive gut they are better able to surmise exactly where their focus is or should be.

They make it a priority to check inward, so to speak. Doing so allows them to determine whether they are focused more on fears of missing out, or losing something instead of having intentions or high expectations of creating, manifesting and experiencing the thing desired.

In other words, they prefer to have a tenacious hold on the feeling of being or experiencing that not yet present thing they desire to have or to be. Even though the thing they desire is not physically present, and they may not have a clue as to how it will all come together, they are not hindered. On the contrary, they continue practicing the feel of it now, as if it is already existing in their present moment.

We usually lump people who can shift their senses inward in this manner within the category of dreamers. But theirs is not the idle fixation of a chronic dreamer. There is substance, depth and inspired action involved with their inner focus. This in turn prompts them to move forward. Not in hopes, but in anticipation, in high expectation!

Note: I do realize that what I've said about having expectations flies contrary to some spiritual guru's advice of having no expectations whatsoever. But let's keep it real. We each hold onto some degree of expectation in life. If not, we wouldn't do much of anything! If I didn't have some type of expectation that eating healthier foods would result in having a more healing, energizing body, or that learning how to operate a specialized tool would better equip me to master a certain skill set, why would I bother to do those things?

Whether or not the thing we desire is for ourselves or others, at some point we expect to have a desire come to fruition. Especially if it's a desire we absolutely believe is possible to attain. I think what often hinders us within the realm of expectations is that we become bound by one means of acquiring a desire. We convince ourselves that our desire can only come about in one or a few limited ways.

However, we should do the complete opposite and expect things to come about in any way imagined or unimagined! We should expect to receive or experience the thing we desire *without* locking ourselves within a certain timeframe or method. This is exactly how great rulers operate. They know with certainty that any next step taken can be the one that places them exactly where they desire to be or better.

Relying on wishful thinking or the crossing of body parts (fingers, eyes, toes, lips) while "hoping" things will somehow work out for the best is not something they do. Neither will they give up if the road to their desire gets a little bumpy, makes a sudden and unexpected turn to the left, or is blocked by some type of obstruction.

No, come what may they have a gut feeling about the outcome being what they desire it to be or more. If or when the road gets bumpy or suddenly turns to the left, they slow down. If they get to a point where the road is blocked, they will either back up or go around the obstruction by finding another route.

From the casual observer's prospective it may appear

that these capable rulers have all of their ducks in a row. It may seem that everything they need in order to realize their dream has already been figured out, collected and labored over. Then, the only thing left for them to do is to put everything in its rightful place.

But more than likely, they will *not* have all the details in place, all of the how's and the when's related to accomplishing their desire. And yet, this doesn't stop them from *feeling* like it is already a done deal because they envision it happening for them so clearly!

They simply go about the act of creatively living while biding their time for the inevitable to occur--the manifestation of their desires. If during the process of manifesting the thing they desire, it begins to feel not quite right for them, they will tweak things within relevant areas until it does. *Or* they will do nothing and wait for the right feelings or answers to come along.

They have experienced this gut feeling phenomenon enough to know that when they go against it, stress over it, ignore or rush it by being fearful, impatient or playing the victim game, the outcome is *not* what they desire. Again, this ability is not just available to the cream of the crop rulers. It's not something only a few are fortunate enough to gain access to and develop. We are each born with this capability.

With the exception of your inner teacher, there is no special club, membership or guru you must exclusively follow in order to be successful in your endeavors. Knowledge and wisdom are not, nor will it ever be limited to one person or group. At the least, it takes an entire Universe! Just know that there is never a time when we do not experience this self-fulfilling, creation phenomenon. Actually, as awesome as it is it's really not a phenomenon at all. It's simply the way we seem designed to be, and the way things are designed to unfold. Nevertheless, many have lost the fine art of how to be it and even how to see it! So yes, with a little applied knowledge we can each develop the ability to better understand and utilize this life building, self-fulfilling creation process—a.k.a. manifesting!

"I had a gut feeling about this one. I knew it wouldn't work but I went through with it anyway!"

How many times have you told yourself and others this very same thing? By the way, my hand is raised and waving too! But I think the bigger question is this. Why do we give things the green light, when we know with certainty that doing so will fail to bring about the desired outcome?

Yes, that was a redundant question because by now you know the answer. It's quite an obvious one. For some odd reason we take great pride in holding on to fear and lack. And again, what we hold on to, what we focus on is what we will experience.

"I was afraid everybody would think I was dumb or not a team player. When it was suggested that I volunteer to tutor math, I agreed even though it's a subject I've always struggled with. Unfortunately, I wasn't much help."

"I could have done it, but I didn't have enough help or the right resources to get the project completed on time. I couldn't manage it alone, so another co-worker was given the task of completing it."

"They locked me up for stealing, but I did those things because I didn't have enough money to buy food, clothes, pay bills and the rent too."

Unlike the hit-or-miss ruler, the aligned and aware ruler learns to better utilize their gut feelings and to engage the optimal side of their coin. That being the love/passion, abundance/I Am side. There's a sense that their success is inevitable even when success doesn't come about easily *or* quickly.

Staying onboard their desire train with thoughts intact, while chug-chugging along until they arrive at their chosen destination is what they do. They don't get all bent out of shape because their desire train has to slow down while negotiating a deep curve, a steep hill or a drastic drop.

Neither do they constantly complain, point the finger or disembark/quit when they're forced to stop at various junctions along the way. They choose to believe that any unexpected stops will not result in wasted energy or time.

Instead, they expect these unplanned stops to provide them with special packages full of valuable life lessons waiting to be picked up and utilized by them. They've learned to make lemonade when they're inundated with an overabundance of lemons!

When enlightened rulers encounter what appears to be opposition, they see new possibilities. In delays, they see an opportunity to make improvements. With setbacks, they see a chance to recharge, rejuvenate and redirect. And with naysayers, they hear absolutely nothing that applies to them!

"Instead of math, I chose to tutor a subject I enjoy and that I'm great at—art! My personal techniques and love of art helped students to appreciate and love art too!"

"I just knew I could complete the assigned project on time. It was a huge undertaking but I was able to collaborate with the best people in order to pull it off!"

"Not having what I've been told I need has ever stopped me from getting what I desire. To some it may have looked impossible for me to rise above certain circumstances, but I knew it could be done. How long it would take was never reason enough for me to give up!"

Don't just take my word for it. Research successful leaders, teachers, small or large business owners, artists or healers and read their bios. Better yet, you can probably talk with some of them in person since you may already know a few of them.

Maybe it's the teenager who does yard work in your neighborhood, or the dependable high schooler who baby sits for you. But what you may not know about them is that they're paying their own way through college, helping with family bills or investing some of their income and creating a nice little nest egg!

If you ask or look for statements referencing how these enlightened, successful rulers are able to do what they do, what you will find over and over again are these three key elements to their success:

1. They possess a **passion and desire** to learn as much as they can about whatever it is they intend to accomplish. Out of ingenuity and less from necessity, some will even become Jack's or Jane's of several trades.

2. They are deeply **inspired to act** on what they **know** *and* **feel**.

3. They are able to **redirect their efforts** and make adjustments when needed.

Now don't get your bloomers all twisted up! Just because you are not in the books doesn't mean you are less exceptional than any other great ruler. Great rulers become so by developing a heightened state of awareness, by cultivating and nourishing their desire to create, express and experience things *and* through repetition. They simply keep doing the things that feel good and works for them. Notice that I didn't say they're prone to picking up their toys and going home at the first hint of opposition or hard work. *Or* that they give up if the process gets a bit uncomfortable and takes more time than they'd calculated.

It is understood and fully accepted by them that opposition may arise, hard work will be required at times, and being a little uncomfortable is only a temporary thing when first entering new and uncharted terrain. What they are able to accomplish is not due to any rocket science capability. Nor are they great rulers because someone or some institution labels them as such.

They focus more on what they love and enjoy being and doing! There's a burning passion inside of them they cannot ignore. Don't you get it? It's not a trick to this gut feeling stuff at all! You simply have to squash your fears, open up, get honest with yourself *about* yourself, stay focused on the thing you desire *and* flexible about how and when it will come to be. Also, be thankful for your learning experiences and realize help is **always** available to you.

No one is ever alone in this process, but and this is a good but. You must learn *how* to ask for things, and it's easier than you think. Trust me ex-gym rat. I got you this far didn't I?

CHAPTER 6

YOUR BEST GUT IS YET TO COME!

Getting what we desire out of life only takes a few steps. But as I stated before, most of us make the process complicated, painful and much longer than it has to be. We get tripped up by ignorance, by the things we don't know as opposed to any level of productive or unproductive activity.

There's the tendency to push, stress and overwork ourselves while aiming for something greatly desired. Or we begin shuffling our feet or tripping over them because we're confused and uncertain of what to do next. Also, if acquiring a desire takes too long, we'll attempt to run, leap or fly before we ever learn how to walk with fearless confidence.

You may have heard the song, *She Works Hard for the Money* by Donna Summer. I once thought this popular disco beat gave kudos to and encouraged all hard-working women. Oops...seems I'm giving you a hint of my ageless eternalness! However, after revisiting the lyrics I've come to this understanding, that it is not a song of encouragement but rather an acknowledgment of the

63

pressures and hardships women sometimes face in life.

What the song failed to mention is the ability of a person to change or rise above an undesirable condition. Had the song made reference to *that* possibility within its catchy lyrics, it would have been a very encouraging, uplifting piece. Still, one can find within these lyrics the opportunity for self-awareness and growth. And yes, here comes another one of my allegories, which you should be use to by now.

Just in case you haven't heard the song before, it spotlights a young woman as she works very hard at an establishment. While there, she forms attachments to some of the clientele as they have taken the time to acknowledge her plight.

She greatly appreciates those who understand what she's going through but ironically, their empathy for her appears to be the very thing she uses to convince herself that she's better off remaining exactly where she is.

It appears that because she is surrounded by those who will commiserate with her about her life condition and choices, she remains loyal to the demanding terms of her profession.

Unfortunately, for twenty-eight years she stays within the same conditions, under the same circumstances. The years go by and she watches people as they come and go. They move on with their lives while she becomes more and more discontent with her own complacency.

Never once does she step outside of her familiar yet painful comfort zone, not even for a chance at improving her situation. The plight of the protagonist in this song is that of many. Too often we choose to stick with the pain or fear we are accustomed to.

To justify these choices, some will belittle or demonize

the idea of even considering a different or unfamiliar approach. As a result, they will immediately (and sometimes permanently) block any chances of encountering a different, much better or slightly improved, imagined or real, wonderful or more tolerable experience or outcome.

Somehow, we convince ourselves not to "tempt fate" and to not summon enough courage to make the desired changes. But I must ask you, which pain trumps? The pain one is currently experiencing, or the idea of a perceived pain that may or may not come about *if* one dares to believe in themselves instead of their circumstances?

As for me, I am of the belief that there's absolutely nothing worth regretting for even one moment, let along twenty-eight years! Why waste additional energy lingering in regrets? The deed has already been done. You cannot undo it, **but** in spite of it, you can progress.

Wouldn't it be better to forgive and let go of the actions that brought about any feelings of regrets? When you do, it will be much easier to uncover any hidden, or to at least acknowledge the obvious lessons concerning the situation.

In this way, one can move smoothly from fears and regrets to making more positive and productive changes. I'll just believe you answered *"Yes!"* to my questions. And because you did, have I got a few excellent life changing lessons for you! I think you'll find them worth acing *and* applying.

Most of these lessons are fairly simple to grasp and to act upon quickly, but a few of you may be a bit uncomfortable with the one I'm about to share next. And no, it's not some off the wall concept or idea.

However, depending on your life experiences and the things you've been taught or told as a child, you may see it as something not worth considering but here it is. You must learn to love, accept and believe in yourself! Yeah, I know what you're thinking right now. *"I already do those things! What are you talking about Yvonne?"*

This is what I'm talking about. In theory most of us *assume* we love, accept and have faith in ourselves, but in practice and under certain circumstances we don't always exhibit self-love or faith.

The self-love I'm referring to is unconditional, forgiving, non-condemning, patient, accepting self-love. It is not ego driven and does not place others above or beneath self. Nor is it demanding of anything, be it praise, power, preference or posturing.

Hopefully, the very same unconditional love and faith you extend to your soul mate, family members, close friends, your religious, academic or occupational affiliations--you are also extending to yourself.

However, I do realize that self-love is not the only love one desires to experience, because being nurtured and loved by another is such a fantastic feeling! As a matter of fact, it's essential for the growth and development of infants to experience nurturing, loving feelings from another.

This loving feeling is greatly desired by just about everyone on the planet. However, with the exception of infants and young children--no one has to love, care for or believe in you **but** you most definitely do!

You shouldn't measure your value by the way others feel or talk about you, be it loving *or* hateful feelings or talk. When you truly begin loving yourself, there's nothing that can sway you from this essential form of self-validation.

Everything you do or consider will be because you love and have faith in yourself just as much as you love and have faith in others. You'll come to understand that you are no more or less deserving than anyone else. Sort of puts everyone on an even keel doesn't it?

When operating within the confines of self-love, you are moved beyond fearing or doubting if you will be deemed worthy. Or that support from a person or group will be withheld.

On the contrary, it will be self-evident that **you** have the authority *and* the ability to initiate changes for your highest good, regardless of how or what others feel or think about you. Also, you'll have no doubts that when needed, assistance will always come.

All it takes is for you to make the smallest of effort, to hold onto the belief of change happening for you, and to never waiver even when it feels and looks like you're not accomplishing very much. You really don't have the luxury of giving up on yourself!

Note: To waiver means to abandon a right or claim. In essence it is the giving up of something. It is by no means the same as having doubts, which will occasionally crop up. Doubts can be excellent early indicators that you are easing out of alignment with your desires, and into alignment with some type of fear.

Try not to get too bent out of shape because it feels like you may be regressing. Doing so will give doubts more strength and staying power. Instead, pay attention to how you're feeling in order to discover what's causing these fears or doubts to pop.

Once you know the cause, politely *and* immediately give those fears their walking papers by debunking and disempowering them. Handle your doubts and then move on. I'll give you more information about how to deescalate fears and doubts later.

Now that you know you should have the utmost confidence and self-love, let's move on to the second step of your manifestation process. Here's where you get to decide the things you really want to experience in life! Yah! This part can be fun, but it can also be overwhelming for some, as there will be the temptation to manifest several things quickly. But trying to manifest too much too quickly can backfire on you.

For one, you will not be able to stay focused any more than a child can when drafting the very best birthday wish list in the entire universe! Especially when their birthday is today. Talk about pressure!

If you attempt to create your desire list in this frame of mind, more than likely you'll end up with this; nothing more tangible than a piece of paper with a bunch of illegible scribble all over it.

To avoid this pitfall, it's very important that you learn how to better focus your intentions, how to maintain or bring back those loving, fearless, stress-free feelings *and* know when to take inspired action. You will not be able to do any of that if you're juggling fifty desires at one time!

The third component to this not so secret manifestation technique is to genuinely express appreciation for the things you have right now.

"Ah…exactly why do I have to show appreciation for the stuff I have but don't want?"

I know *you* didn't ask that question, but I'll answer it. For starters, your appreciation isn't limited to material stuff only. There's so much more than that to be grateful for. Extend your gratefulness to those life experiences and lessons learned, *especially* the difficult to recognize or to understand ones.

"Yvonne, this is not helping me feel any better about appreciating stuff I don't want!"

Again, I know *you* didn't make that statement. But for

those who may have, consider the following as a reason for being appreciative. Those difficult experiences will be the very ones jammed packed with valuable, life enhancing information for you and others.

Unfortunately, we tend to measure the value of our blessings against the perceived value of others blessings. And quite often, from our measuring stick, theirs can appear to be far greater or lesser than ours!

For example. Just because your new Ford Fiesta is small, (personally I think they're cute and have excellent gas mileage) it does get you from point A to point B just as your neighbor's new Super Duty Ford Extended Cab Pickup does. Their vehicle is bigger, more powerful and expensive, *but* is no better than yours at getting you where you want to go!

On the flip side, we don't often compare our blessings or lessons against others blessings we have valued as far less than ours. Like the friend who can't afford a car and must walk, ride a bike or bus everywhere they need to go, and in all types of weather.

If the proverbial car is now in the others garage, can you imagine them turning their nose up at the ease it will be to have a new Ford Fiesta at their disposal? Especially after having to walk, catch a ride or a bus to get everywhere they need or want to be? If they did such a thing, it would be the epitome of ungratefulness!

Ungratefulness is a total disregard for others who have played a part, no matter how small or large, in helping you to manifest the things you desire. No one manifests anything all by themselves. Though it is the individual's initial desire that begins the process, others help bring it to fruition. Please don't become the big headed one who starts believing it's all their doing. It's not!

Never kick your gifts, lessons and those helpful others to the curb as if they're not relevant or useful. They will always be both. Being grateful for the things you have received doesn't mean you can't strive for better or more if better or more is what you desire.

The simple gesture of appreciation, especially when you are within your pre-manifestation stage, demonstrates that you are capable of handling more. You're ready for a new life experience increase!

Remember, whether difficult or easy, desired or not, all your experiences can be used to help move you forward and towards any goal or desire. You are always moving from one experience to the next anyway, so why not learn to make the best of any experience?

As a matter of fact, why not place all your experiences under the litmus test. In this way, you'll be better able to recognize if you are complicating or simplifying a situation, or manifesting something undesired instead of something yearned for.

Let's say you focus more on being happy, excited about life or the next adventure. You make the decision to hold onto ever good feeling, thought or talk and in the process, you come to realize that aside from a few rocky experiences, things are going as you've envisioned or better.

This is a definite indication that your life litmus indicator is the color of clear blue water. You are definitely within the cool, calming flow of a life that's pleasing to you! But then one day you somehow lose your good feeling focus.

You begin to concentrate more on people, events or conditions outside of your control. As you listen to and take on the concerns of others, you start believing you must do things to please or help everybody while placing yourself on the back burner that's turned off.

What happens next is as avoidable as it is predictable. Feelings of unhappiness, fear, blame, anger, impatience or victimization becomes overwhelming, and nothing seems to be going your way.

When this is your experience, the color of your life litmus indicator is hot lava red. You are a hot, smoking mess and have placed yourself under so much internal pressure until your life is on the verge of imploding or erupting!

If you find yourself within this volatile, magmatic flow of discontent and negativity, it means you are desperately struggling within and blocking yourself from that which you truly desire to experience. So, let's get unblocked, calm and happy again!

Now calm yourself, get centered and take a few deep breaths then scale your desires down to one or two things you believe will be easy to accomplish. Don't attempt to tackle the big stuff just yet as you have more resistance to those big-ticket items coming about.

For instance, if you don't have a significant other yet, hold off on planning that Prince Charming or Cinderella wedding for now. The same goes for starting a new 100k a month income generating business. It's doable, but if you're struggling to manage 2K a month, focus more on stabilizing and then incrementally increasing your current income before attempting to manifest such a vast number of Benjamins!

Once you form the habit of calmly, clearly and consciously practicing the art of manifesting a few smaller in resistance desires, a trickledown or cup running over effect occurs. Other desires and even things you didn't think were desires at all but fleeting thoughts or wishes, will seem to manifest with little to no effort on your part.

Why? Because you will have initiated the necessary inner work which then opens those once blocked channels and allows abundance to flow into your life unimpeded by self-doubt and worries. Can you think of a better motivator for remaining clear, relaxed and open to your desires manifesting then to have abundance falling all over you from every direction? I'm also referring to directions or means you didn't even know about!

Come on now, you have to admit that's pretty awesome. And what's even better about this type of built in high-octane encouragement is that it will enable (embolden) you to go for the most daunting, allusive desire of them all. The Big Kahuna!

Admit it, your number one desire has probably been on your life experiences wish list for many years. For as long as you have been desiring it, I'm sure at times it seemed just as cunning and slippery as the legendary big fish that always manages to wiggle away.

But this doesn't have to happen anymore. That is, if you change your fishing technique. When you do, there'll be no more fighting against the big one. It will actually seem as if it wants to be caught and that's because it does!

Your big or little one is meant for no one except you! It has been waiting patiently for you to calm down, to stop rocking the boat and getting your desire line tangled up in fears and doubts.

Soon after you become calm and clear, you will be able to reel it in and easily scoop it up with your net of expectations. Then the only thing left for you to do will be to baste in your adventure, bring home that fine catch, and feast on it for breakfast, lunch, dinner *and* dessert!

Yes, there is a fish dessert, I looked it up. It's made with honey, brown sugar, coconut flakes and salmon. Well...I'm sure it tastes sweet, so it could be a dessert. Dessert or not, you'll at least have a new and exciting story to tell. And this time it will be about the big one you actually caught! But remember, that's just your first big catch. You can always add more to your life experiences wish list.

There's no limit or cap on the things you can think, imagine or desire unless you somehow manage to stop thinking, imagining possibilities and desiring new experiences. In my opinion this is highly unlikely to happen. So, go ahead and take your time deciding which desires you'd like to work on first. I've got all day. I'm not going anywhere.

You may not have thought much about this before but your desires are quite common, universal in fact. People worldwide desire the same things. I'm sure you've guessed that security is at the top of this universal desire list and can come in various forms.

Due to the fact that we live in a monetary system, money is by far the top security inducer. What usually follows money is shelter, nourishment, health, the perfect partner or co-creators to share one's life with. Or it can be something as simple as a safe and reliable car.

If you think about it, all of the things I mentioned (but hopefully with the exception of a perfect partner) requires money to obtain them. And whereas you may be given or barter for some of these things, rest assured it took some type of monetary exchange in order to produce the things that were eventually passed on to you.

I've mentioned how money is used and needed because some tend to fear or downplay this important tool. Money is most definitely a tool, much like those used by a carpenter, an artist or a gardener. The tool is never the problem, even if it breaks down or becomes obsolete. But the one welding it, or the one who is responsible for creating and maintaining it is usually where or with whom most of the problems originate.

Personally, I don't know of anyone, be they a master or hobbyist, and who enjoys or has made a livelihood from an activity, to be intimidated or afraid of acquiring and using tools. Envision a hammer for carpentry, a paint brush for painting or pruners for gardening. These tools are essential for creating the things one intends to enjoy and share with others.

Doesn't it seem unrealistic to fear a tool? Especially when considering that a tool, of its own volition cannot help or hinder you. Isn't it more beneficial to be aware of your intentions for using a tool, be it money, a computer or a phone?

However, we don't always desire physical things in which a tool may be required to produce it. Sometimes we prefer more intangible internal things like peace of mind, higher awareness, more knowledge, emotional stability, fearlessness or spiritual growth. It really doesn't matter what you desire as long as you believe it's possible for you to have it.

Now this is just a heads up from sista' Jones, but if you are seeking something you know will harm others, or adds zero value to anyone, I caution you against desiring that. Be mindful of what you ask for and how you go about getting it.

Therefore, beneficial or not, inconsequential or monumental, the thing you passionately seek will most definitely seek you. The Law of Reciprocity--what goes around comes around, is the ultimate universal check and balance system in place that alerts us of any beneficial or unbeneficial actions we choose to perform.

Can't say I didn't warn you. What you throw out there (your thoughts, feelings and actions) has an astounding way of coming back to hit ya! Okay, I've done my moral duty.

Now that you've made up your mind about the top one or two things you want to acquire or accomplish, write them down. Be specific but brief. Include what you desire, (car, money, mate, house) how you desire it to be (amount, color, size, brand) and the general time frame you would like to receive it.

After you've written down your desire, read it out loud. Once will be enough. Since there's no time like the present and because your desires are so vivid and fresh in your mind, why not grab a pen and paper and get started now? I'll wait.

How did it feel when you read it out loud? Was it believable enough to make you smile, or did it make you a little uncomfortable? Did it feel possible or impossible? In the back of your mind, could you hear yourself say something along these lines?

"Yes, this is possible. With a little help in the right direction, I can do this!" Or was it more like this? *"Yeah, nope! Ain't gonna' happen!"*

Don't panic if the reaction to your statement was less than positive. Whichever response you had was the correct one because that's how you feel and think at the moment. This little exercise simply shows where you currently stand within your belief arena. Especially when the spotlight is shining on your main desire.

Okay, here's what I need you to do next and I must warn you beforehand, this will be difficult for some. Are you ready? Take that piece of paper, the one with your detailed desires, the things you've meticulously and joyfully written down as must haves, and rip or ball it up! Yes, that's exactly what I'm asking you to do with it.

Brace yourself because you're about to get *very* upset with me. Here's what you **must** do next. Stand up, walk to the nearest trash can, and drop those ripped or balled up dreams inside of it. Go ahead, you're strong enough to do this, and I'm strong enough to handle what you're thinking and saying about me right now.

"No she didn't! Is she for real? Why the heck did she get me all excited about the things I want, trick me into reliving all that good stuff, and then have the unmitigated gall to ask me to toss my dreams in the can?"

Guilty as charged. However, as much as I do not enjoy being the bearer of unpleasant news, that's exactly what you've been doing with the desires you'd love to experience but haven't as yet. You've been ripping them apart and tossing the remnants of them in the *"I can't have this now!"* reject receptacle of your mind. Not only have you shredded and trashed them once, you've done it repeatedly! Go ahead and admit it!

No one is beyond reproach or can hold it against you if you've created more vision boards than you care to remember. So what if you've made long detailed wish-lists, repeated in astronomical numbers every affirmation known to man, *and* informed everyone within earshot what you were "hoping" for. Who's in a position to judge you?

Here's another question for you. Did any of the activity I just mentioned produce anything for you? If you are like some, those who seem to stumble upon a result, then you may have realized a portion of your desires before getting stuck in limbo again.

But if you are like many who often become stalled within their pre-manifestation stage, not one single aspect of the thing you truly desired came about. I know exactly how that feels. Those very same activities left me scratching my head and wondering what I'd done wrong, since the thing I wanted most had yet to manifest. Some things would manifest, but it was not the thing at the top of my list, the thing I desired with all my heart.

However, by now you may have come to realize I'm a bit on the stubborn side. If it's something I truly desire then I don't give up on it! I keep searching either actively or passively, because I know the answers are out there somewhere. And sure enough, they always are. Do you want to know what I found out? I realized I had to let my desires go. Uh…did I just hear you scream?

"No way am I giving up my desires!"

Well, good for you! But the thing you most definitely have to give up is stressing over the idea that your desires are MRA, Missing Regardless of Action. Here's the thing. What we actually get all stressed out and beat ourselves up about is not the desire itself, because we are deeply in love with the thought of a desire. But we tend to narrow our focus on the temporary appearance of it not currently being evident.

We then have a complete faith breakdown or turn around, because that which we so passionately desire is not present, not tangible, we cannot touch it or see it. In fact, it's taking its own sweet time about getting to us, and we can't even imagine how on Earth it will ever come to be. So, what's the point! Whew! Sounds just like your everyday run of the mill temper tantrum or pity party doesn't it?

"I never get what I want!" *"I'm just not* (fill in the blank) *good, smart or talented enough!"* or *"Everybody, even the Institution is against me!"*

Unfortunately, it is this type of thinking that we overindulge in and attach to our beloved desires. Which subsequently keeps our desires away, and instead brings to us those feared things we are so adamantly asking for.

Oh, you think you're not asking for, correction--demanding all the crappy stuff you keep getting? Let's take a closer look at these crippling "belies" a.k.a. beliefs we tend to reinforce on a constant basis.

"I never get what I want!" Really? You have not ever in your lifetime received **anything** you've wanted? Never?

"I'm just not good, smart or talented enough!"

Hmm. Well, I know of a few folks who by social standards were deemed not good, smart or talented enough and yet they were able to get what they wanted, at least some of the time. So why not you? Could it be that getting what you desire has nothing whatsoever to do with being good, smart or talented enough?

Sidebar: I'm just curious, but how does one quantify what degree of goodness, intelligence or talent is enough to have when it applies to getting what they desire? And last but not yeast:

"Everybody, even the Institution is against me!"

If this is true, you would have to be the most known and disagreeable person in the entire world for everybody to know and then go against you. Even the Institution, who sees us as numbers on a flow chart and couldn't possibly "know" us, knows *you?* That's quite impressive, also a bit scary but impressive, nevertheless.

Please don't think I'm being insensitive by bringing these false beliefs (belies) and statements to your attention. I'm direct sometimes, but never insensitive. I simply want to impress upon you how entertaining such thoughts is the main thing that blocks you from experiencing your desires.

We don't care for these hurtful thoughts at all, and yet we spend much more energy engaging with them than we do with our beloved desires. And we wonder why our desires are not with us. Crazy, uh? I understand how me asking you to stop stressing over them can feel like you're giving them up, but of course you're not.

The thing you are giving up is the fear of your desires remaining just out of your reach. Therefore, it will cost you more head and stomach aches if you don't stick with the initial suffering as proof that you are worthy of receiving what you ask for. *That's* the thinking and feeling you must give up.

You don't have to suffer to prove yourself worthy or to acquire anything. But if you are to give up those old unproductive trains of thoughts and feelings, then you must replace them with more beneficial, uplifting, inspiring, happy, heart-thumping thoughts and feelings.

You will have to create trains of thought that make you smile and laugh, or hum and sing, or do a little ditty when you think about them. In essence, you'll have to release the fear, lack of faith, self-pity and impatience you have inadvertently connected to your desires.

Getting rid of all your treacherous thoughts and stinky speaking is essential. Because now you know hanging out with that bunch is only making you feel horrible, and drawing nothing but misery into your life. They are not your friends so dump them!

After you've dumped that crew, you can start paying more attention to your true friends--love, excitement, giggly anticipation, peaceful patience and vivid imagery. These are the very best friends to ever come your way, and you know this because it feels so good when you're kicking it with them!

From this point on, you will learn to custom design your very own **M**otivational **A**ction **P**hrases, or MAP as I like to call it. If done correctly, your MAP will help you move past the uneventful, disempowering location of point A. This is the place you'd love to move beyond because you are no longer realizing your full potential there.

Instead, your MAP will help to move you towards the all inspiring, ever evolving, loving location of point Z. This is the place you truly desire to be in route to, because setting your sights forward and towards this destination is where all those wonderful potentials in life await you!

Yes, you must learn to write your very own happy now and ever after, no matter what comes your way, never ending love story *and* feel as if you're living that wonderful life right now! Okay? Now, let's work on bringing your MAP to life.

Should your MAP has anything to do with money, but does not resonate with you, then maybe the amount is too high or too low, or the time frame is too long or too short. Play around with it until it sounds and feels more like an inevitable event occurring for you. If you don't believe, agree with or have faith in the words that are coming from your own thoughts or mouth, how can you expect anybody or anything else to?

Your MAP should push all of your fearless inspired action buttons, get you excited, help you visualize living your goals as you're patiently waiting for them to manifest. It should help to reawaken all the possibilities in life, all the wonderful what if's and those worry-free why not's! Sounds like some mighty powerful mojo doesn't it? Yet if you can remember, you've done this often as a child.

As children we were able to open a book or watch our favorite show, and lose ourselves within those pages or that flickering screen. We became fully involved with the adventure. So much so, until it felt like we were there happily engaging with our favorite heroes or delivering a much-needed attitude adjustment to the villain of the day.

This is exactly the way you must get involved with your own life story! However, yours is not a story constructed with mere ink, paper or film. Nor is it created and written for the entertainment of others. As fantastic as it may seem and whether happily or not, moment by moment you are imagining, creating, scripting and telling the life story you are presently living. And for as long as you are here existing, you will continue to do just that.

Now, please don't take what I'm about to say next in the wrong way. I am by no means minimizing anyone's life experiences, *but* if you are not happy with the life story you're living, then why not rewrite it? It's really as simple as deciding to pick up a pencil, flipping it back and forth between the lead and eraser so you can remove, edit and add to your life script as you see fit.

Your life is meant to be an interesting, ongoing, knuckle-biting, page-turning, constantly evolving, living story packed full of every possible experience there is for you to imagine having and more. That's what living is or should be!

Wait a minute…let's just take a count. For those of you who want nothing more than to muddle along in a life full of fears, uncertainties and unawareness while holding fast to the idea that you have absolutely no control over what happens to you…**ever**, please raise your hand.

Woo! I can't tell you how happy I am to *not* see a hand waving in the air! I'm ecstatic to see that you recognize the potential of your empowerment, and that you are not a victim in or of life. Kudos to you for slipping on your Super Being suit! And I must say, you wear it well. ☺

Within all the living stories we part-human beings' script

and reenact, there is always a beginning, a middle and an ending of a chapter. And since we'll dealing with one chapter at a time, we can make that chapter as epic or as brief as we choose.

With that being the case, there's no legitimate reason why we should remain hesitate at the very beginning of our life story's first, second or third chapter because of uncertainties.   Neither should we be resolved to remaining stalled by chronic worries in the middle of a chapter, or afraid of approaching the ending of one. At any given moment we can change the tone, the feel, the message, the expectations of a current chapter, or easily add a new one! So, shouldn't we get on with it?

Remember, as soon as you suited up, that action meant your refusal to perform any acts of victimhood, and that no matter what's currently written in the script, your new role is to be happy and consciously aware while performing center stage in the story of your life!

Is it just me, or do you sense the excitement of living a life by design instead of by default? Yeah...you do! I'm envisioning you bobbing your head up and down again.   So enough with the questions, no more burning daylight. Let's get on with this show, let's do this!

CHAPTER 7

YOU DON'T HAVE TO CHASE
THE RABBIT TO GET THERE

By now you must know that each individual is responsible for creating the life they desire to experience. While you are in the process of creating and living a life desired, you'll have experiences that will come easily and be enjoyable. During those times you may feel as if you're dancing or skipping along a golden brick road.

There will also be challenging, unpleasant or painful experiences in which you'll find yourself far off the beaten path with scarcely a trail left to follow. Naturally, because of its ease and pleasantry, some will argue that the golden brick road is much better than the dirt trail that peters out.

But I have come to realize you can't always judge a path by its bricks *or* dirt. The path which peters out tends to provide the impetus for one to find a new and often better path. It has always been through the forging of difficult paths where I've gained my most valuable insights and is the reason I'm sharing with you now.

It was while navigating one such dirt trail when I discovered a hidden manifestation block. It was a benign, unpretentious appearing influencer but because of my eventual awareness of it, I was able to instantly understand how it had affected me through the years. To say that I was blown away by what I'd discovered would be an understatement. But let's talk about blocks in general and then I'll go over the personal block I discovered and released.

When it comes to blocks, they are usually the result of some childhood influence/suggestion that was verbally or physically reinforced over the years. These suggestions were often given by well-meaning parents, caretakers, teachers, friends or peers who were oblivious of their negative connotations.

Some of the most common influencers pertaining to money blocks stem from statements such as the following:

Said to child: *"Money doesn't just fall out of the sky! Sometimes you have to do things you don't want to do to get it!"*
Felt by child: *It's scary and very hard to get money.*
Said to child: *"We can't afford that!"*
Felt by child: *I can't have what I want.*
Said to child: *"You have to work harder than that!"*
Felt by child: *I can't do it.*
Said to child: *"All rich people are greedy and selfish!"*
Felt by child: *People will not like me if I have things?*
Said to child: *"You can't have everything you want!"*
Felt by child: *I shouldn't ask for things?*

Then there are suggestions that don't appear to contribute to us developing blocks at all. More than likely, they were intended to be sympathetic or encouraging statements to sooth any disappointments or hurts we experienced. But in their subtleness, they can be just as damaging, if not more so than suggestions that are direct and to the point. For example:

Said to child: *"I know you tried, but no one will blame you if you quit!"*
Felt by child: *I should give up. Why even try.*
Said to child: *"It's not much, but it will have to do!"*
Felt by child: *I can't do anything right.*
Said to child: *"Sometimes good things just don't come your way!"*
Felt by child: *Will I ever be good enough?*
Said to child: *"Don't worry about it, you're not the only one who has failed at this!"*
Felt by child: *I'm a failure?*

Sometimes it is not the words spoken to us, but the actions we feel are directed at us that can create blocks. Like a smirk or frown, a look of disappointment or anger, someone turning their back toward you or slamming a door in your face. Even something as simple as a person walking away and not acknowledging you can cause a block.

If these actions are demonstrated often enough and sometimes once is enough, then blocks can develop. It's quite understandable why one chooses to avoid situations that have the potential to bring about an undesired reaction. Especially if the reaction comes from a person they care about.

Whether we've perceived correctly or misread the intentions of others, our inborn flight/avoidance or fight/protection responses kick in. We'll either attempt to avoid the situation all together, or take measures to shield ourselves from any perceived unpleasantness. My personal experience of manifesting a money block was much different from the influencers/suggestions I just mentioned, and was the reason I found it so difficult to identify.

As a child, neither of my parents nor did any other adults within my clan or circle inundate me with disempowering, success blocking statements about money. You can just imagine how frustrating it was for me to have a money block in which I didn't fit the criteria for. From what I was told the most common triggers were, I shouldn't have had a money block at all, but I did!

Allow me to clarify that this was not a chronic block. It was not hell bent on following me around like an adorable lost puppy I should **never** have fed! If you're a dog lover, I'm sure you know it's almost impossible to shake a fed puppy.

However, and I'm sure many of you can attest to this as well, the block had a knack for popping up at the most inconvenient times. It was very frustrating for me, but I knew there had to be a way to discover and deconstruct this cleverly hidden block.

I also sensed that it would probably be located in a memory, a belief that I felt was safe and because I couldn't see it, someone outside of my past and present would have to help me find it. It was, and they did. While participating in a training that focused on blocks in general but which branched off to money blocks specifically, participants were instructed to revisit their childhood.

Pertaining to money blocks, we were instructed to observe how parents, care takers and other influential adults dealt with money. How they would share, spend or save, talk or not talk about money was to be noted. We were to pay very close attention as to how it felt while observing them interact with money. And although I didn't think it

would reveal anything new, I went along with the process.
The following are excerpts of what I remembered:

*"As a child I sensed from my parents the importance of work, of
earning income in order to have the basic necessities in life, and that
having the basics—food, shelter, clothing, protection from harm, plus a
few wants every now and then was good enough and something to be
thankful for. And I was thankful for having those basic necessities
met because I did feel very safe, loved and protected.*

*Because I felt cared for in every way, it was easy to accept that
having those life sustaining basics was in fact enough, and that it was
a good thing. Everything was okay. Besides, how could I have even
imagined to complain or feel at odds with having my needs met?
Especially when my parents seemed so willing to share with me those
needs which facilitated a happy, stable life.*

*Never once do I remember them complaining about not having
enough for themselves, whether it was time, energy, money or things.
Neither did I witness any angry exchanges concerning money (or
anything else) between the two of them.* [Digressing from notes. If
you know old school parents, they wouldn't dare discuss
their "business" around children who can't hold water, let
alone their tongue! So that **never** happened. Back to my
notes.]

*However, sometimes I did sense a certain level of anxiety from
them, but at the time I wasn't sure what it was. I was just too young
to figure it out. Now I completely understand. As most parents do,
they sometimes worry about adequately providing for their family.*

*Still, as a child with a limited understanding of how our unique
family dynamics worked, I somehow knew not to demand things for
myself that cost too much. I guess not being a demanding pain in the
butt was my special contribution to the family.* [Digressing from
notes again. This was very easy for me to do because there
wasn't a lot of stuff I felt I had to have. I still feel this way.
Back to my notes.]

I'm so fortunate and thankful my parents had good work and family ethics they passed down, and that they did an excellent job caring and providing for the family. I'm very thankful to have had them for parents, and I completely understand that neither my parents nor could I have foreseen the negative side effects of accepting such a limiting idea as the following: Having one's basic needs met, and maybe a little extra every now and then is enough.

[Digressing from notes again. This realization hit me like a ton of bricks! It had been so subtle prior to me uncovering it. Had I not followed the simple instructions given to me, and taken the time to calmly and patiently reflect on my childhood, I may have never seen it!

This discovery also led me to recall my thoughts as an adult concerning having just enough while pow-wowing with other parents. I now cringe when remembering those conversations. The fact that I'd somehow convinced myself to *ever* settle for being dead broke after handling all family responsibilities simply boggles my mind! Back to my notes.]

This having just enough concept was most certainly a money paradigm handed down to my parents. They both grew up just after the time of the great depression, a time which required diligent frugality. They simply didn't know any other way, and they certainly didn't think it was harmful. But now that I am aware and better understand this family money paradigm I've been holding onto, I can change it.

I can correct this error in thinking that just getting by, just having my basic needs met and maybe a little more every now and then is enough. I can change the belief that working harder to "just get by" is acceptable and is something I have to do.

This new understanding and awareness does not diminish the fact that I am grateful for the things I have now. It simply means I no longer believe that the things I have today will be as much as I can

*expect to have tomorrow. I can have as much as I desire, and it's
okay to have more than just enough. There's absolutely nothing wrong
with desiring and receiving more!*

*From this pivotal point of awareness, I intend to develop a different
attitude about abundance, that there is much more than just enough for
me to envision having. I'm talking about millionaire mind-set,
millionaire abundance, millionaire giving, millionaire love of life. Yes,
I'm open to receiving all of that and then some!*

I now choose to experience abundance in **every** *area of my life.
I'm open to all the way's abundance will flow to me, because I'm an
awesome being and I totally deserve it! No one can shine like I can.
My light is my light and I love sharing this ever evolving and
increasing light that is in me, that is me!"* Hey, sometimes you
gotta' be your own cheerleader! End of notes to self.

Once I had this revelation and felt certain that I was in
agreement with the concept, I knew I'd never again have to
chase that allusive prosperity rabbit head first down a never
ending empty black hole! Neither would I have to overturn
every hard and heavy rock I might stumble upon in life, or
peer deeply into any or all dark, troubling circumstances I
may encounter over the years.

Doing those things would have only ended with me
falling deeper down an endless hole of fear and indecision.
I would have come to dread the process. Is there anything
beneficial about a process that offers more of the same
stuff one is already experiencing—fear, dread and
confusion? No, there isn't.

Out of my search for this once hidden money paradigm,
I have come to realize three very important things. One,
that I should always calmly, fearlessly and without filters,
look within to find the answers. Ultimately, that's where all
the answers are. Two, I must follow up and respond to
these answers with inspired action. Three, to **never, ever**

forget this simple process!

I'm sure you are familiar with or have studied some of the world's great spiritual teachers. Every single one of these great teachers have instructed, even gone as far as pleading with us to go within when seeking answers.

However, you will have to let go of some outer junk (filters) in order to find your way inside. I'll share some ways in which to do that in a bit, but let's get back to that money block.

Prior to me becoming more aware of the principles related to abundance, some affirmation statements practiced by other's were simply not believable for me. Like most, I couldn't convince myself to believe a thing to be a reality if it was not exhibiting itself fully in my physical world or understanding.

For example, I was so not believing the statement, *"I'm a millionaire!"* when I knew for a fact that $2.75 was in my bank account. The logical part of me would kick in because $2.75 was nowhere near millionaire money in my checkbook ledger!

However, I have learned that how I feel and what I know about certain aspects of a desire, coupled with the correct/resonating wording of any related life building statement *will* make it believable for me.

While I am not a millionaire (money wise) *yet*, I know that it's possible for not only myself but for anyone to become one. I had to drop my clogged filters, those old limiting, unreliable assumptions, opinions, attitudes and ideologies concerning money. At that point in my awareness, it would have been a form of insanity to keep holding onto them!

Think about it. It doesn't seem to matter if one comes from very affluent or humble beginnings, extremely difficult or fortunate circumstances, is a scoundrel or a saint. Either can accomplish the very same goal. The goal being, experiencing abundance in any chosen form! Sort of brings home the statement, *"God (Source, The Universe) is no respecter of persons,"* doesn't it? All is favored *if* they desire and is open (in agreement) to being favored!

I have come to understand that I'm a millionaire in other ways and that the job or stock market, winning Texas lotto ticket, family inheritance or benevolent strangers are *not* the only source of my millionairness. You do know that millionairness is another word I made up, right? All of the things I've mentioned are simply channels for abundance to flow *to* me.

My source comes from within. It is the Infinite, God, the Universe, the Unlimited I Am. It is the creative energy force which thinks things into existence. And together, we (Source and each of us) are co-creators flowing within this vast energy stream of creativity.

Did you happen to notice I said flowing within and not struggling without? Can you wrap your mind around knowing instead of doubting and naysaying your ability to flow *with* the Source of an all-encompassing abundance?

Setting one's intention to go *with* the flow, being open and thereby allowing any channels of abundance to directly pour into one's life is the best way to flow in my opinion. There's really little point in hedging all our bets on a few iffy, finite channels when God/Source has the hookup to an unlimited number of them!

It may appear as a mystery to some, but it happens quite often. There are those who are open enough and willing to become inspired. They then take the appropriate actions (be it physical, emotional or spiritual) while also holding onto the expectation of known *and* unknown forces assisting them in drawing a desire into their present state of being.

Success is always the result when we combine this simple approach to realizing any goal or desire. I'm not sure if you've taken the time to notice this but there are indeed forces that work exclusively for our benefit. Yes, I'm being somewhat frivolous because surely you know this already.

Some of these forces work in the foreground as people or things we are aware of. Such as employers, employees, a significant other, the devices we use to receive and convey information, or the automobile one drives every day. We personally know of, see and interact with these people or things often.

Others will work in the background, as people or things we do not personally know of. They can be the hospital's lab technician or the machine that sorts mail. More than likely, we will never see or physically interact with them as they are performing these tasks for us. However, we know they exist because we understand the way lab work and mail is processed. When completed, the results of our lab work are received and once sorted, mail is delivered. And we get these things whether we want them or not!

Then there are those other forces which seem to operate at entirely different levels—not quite human or mechanical. It's a level some are unaccustomed to acknowledging or uninterested in knowing much about.. We don't fully understand these forces and some don't believe they exist at all. Yet somehow, they are revealed to us through a means we can sense. In other words, we have a "gut" feeling, an intuitive sense of their presence and involvement.

These unknown forces can appear and assist us in many ways—as new concepts, thoughts and ideas, flashes of insight and visions or dreams. But they are not limited by our thought perceptions or interpretations. They can also be realized through tangible, auditory and visual means as well.

Most of us have some degree of an awareness concerning all three of the forces I've mentioned. We know they work or come about in various ways, but they can sometimes be beyond our physical ability to see and to manipulate, or to fully understand.

In our everyday lives we rely on a number of unseen forces/channels to help keep us safe, to provide for and even entertain us, yet we never question those. When you turn the key in your Chrysler 300 ignition, do you worry about the hood warming up like that of a Kenmore Cooktop oven?

Have you ever thought your local store would stop providing all milk products simply because farmer Brown from Little Known Cow Town USA, decided not to coax ole Bessie out of her milk the day before? How about your favorite radio station, ever wonder if those radio waves will bounce from the ionosphere and then get picked up so you can jam the box?

Again, I'll answer those for you. No, no and no! I'm even willing to bet the farm (pun intended again) that most of you have never thought about such things until I mentioned them. While I've given you examples of a few forces we can easily manipulate and control, there are others in which we part-humans have little to no control over whatsoever.

However, it could be we're simply unaware that we can control or manipulate them. For example, how our planet rotates and tilts with such precision is believed to be beyond our ability to orchestrate. The maintenance of this perfect balancing act is the reason our sun, moon and stars appear to rise, set or fall on their own accord.

Ever deeply contemplate why moisture gathers itself up from the ground and bodies of water only to drop back down to Earth as rain, snow or hail, repeating the cycle over and over again? Yes, as you well know science, philosophy and religion gives us an explanation for these occurrences. But when, how or what set all this in motion *and* maintains it, is to this very day still hotly debated.

Whether there's a sound explanation or not, we believe in all of these things because we experience them routinely. As a matter of fact, we set our time (hours of the day, seasons, etc.) by these super-naturally reoccurring events.

We know they exist or can be made to exist even though we may not understand exactly how they have come to be. Quite frankly, most of us are not the least bit concerned with how the things we desire, need and use on a daily basis are created. It's already done for us. We don't get all tripped up about it, we just go with it. Why reinvent a perfectly functioning wheel? Right?

Well, it's a good thing we don't have to reinvent the wheel, but every now and then some of us wouldn't mind having a set of custom-built ones. This is why you may want to consider becoming a cartographer and creating your very own personal MAP.

In your uniquely created map will be all the specifications and directions you will need for acquiring those new and shiny special built wheels you're expecting to receive!

CHAPTER 8

Your Engine, Chassis and Map

Have you ever stopped to consider what happens inside your head and body whenever you ask yourself a basic question? I know you probably haven't. Sometimes we ignore the things we think, say and do because our thoughts and actions are usually scattered all over the place! For example:

"What did I do with those keys?" or *"Why did I come in this room?"*

Good question given it was a mere second ago when you held those keys in your hand, or knew exactly where you were going and why. So, what happened to you between a second ago and now?

Maybe a prankster poltergeist hid your keys, or some other entity took temporary possession of your body because it needed to be in a certain room in your house. You don't really believe that, do you? I hope not because here's a better explanation.

Your thoughts were hopping all over the place while your body was on auto pilot. Ta-da! Mystery solved. This is what tends to happen when we are not presently connected with our thoughts, feelings and actions, which subsequently blocks us from access to certain things like recall or presence!

Now let's go deeper. What did you instantly do after asking yourself either one of those questions? For the times when I've temporarily misplaced something or walked into a room without a clue, the very first thing I did was to stop moving all together, or to at least slow down. I slowed down physically *and* mentally.

Not only did I slow down, it felt as if I were attempting to peel back the layers and take a peek inside my brain. I wanted to review the activities I had performed prior to losing something, or walking into a room without remembering why.

What I was actually doing was bringing myself back to attentiveness, to being more aware and in a present state of being. I was getting back into a mindset that was more focused on what my initial intention had been concerning what I was thinking and wanted to do.

This is how our higher self/higher consciousness works, except it's much better at it since it doesn't lose track of desires, intention or inspiration. Nor is time, ease, difficulty or labels such as good or bad ever a factor.

Our higher consciousness functions at a different level—fully aware and fully present. Whereas it appears to work in conjunction with the brain and body, it also seems to be separate from all the routine ramblings and knee-jerk responses we often perform as we navigate through life.

By seeing or knowing the all-encompassing bigger picture, higher consciousness is able to not just connect with but to be the best response to any question asked. Yeah, we've got all of that awesomeness working on our behalf!

However, we can only realize these better responses when we get out of our own way and allow the response to come through. And as I said before, to receive the best answers we need to ask the best questions with the corresponding feelings attached. Example:

Disempowering question: *"Why am I so dumb?"*

Empowering question: *"How do I become more aware and knowledgeable every day?"*

Now, I'm no brain scientist, but I'm pretty sure that constantly asking yourself why you are the thing you don't want to be only reinforces, supports, advances the thing you don't want! What I believe our brain does when we ask ourselves any question is to look for past experiences of any actions related to the question.

Our brain acts much like a computer in a car's engine except it out performs any manmade computer in existence. The gray matter encased within our skull not only regulates and supports bodily functions--organs, temperature and the regeneration of blood, bone and tissue, it also monitors our thoughts and emotions.

When you ask with such heartfelt passion, *"Why am I so dumb?"* the only thing your brain can pull up for you (and it will do so quick, fast and in a hurry) are the actions *you* have categorized as dumb—all of them!

The stronger the emotional experience is concerning any event in your life, your brain will code that experience as something extremely important and thereby place it on high priority, amber alert status!

In other words, you can relive this past experience and it will feel to you as if it is currently happening. It does not matter to the brain if what you are seeking is something pleasant or unpleasant as it is only responding to your feelings, thoughts and speech—these are all your commands. Recalling and reliving any damaging hurtful stuff is not the least bit helpful, and yet we do it all the time because we are ignorant as to how words, thoughts and feelings actually shape or miss-shape our world.

Most people find it hard to believe they maintain greater focus on the things they do not desire as opposed to the things that they do. They have convinced themselves that what they are doing is being "realistic" about what is.

Sure, one can realistically affirm as to whether or not they acquired the thing they desired last week or last year. But many tend to assume that because they are not seeing evidence of a different outcome at the present moment, an undesired past experience is destined to reoccur instead.

Since what is desired has yet to come about, some become convinced that an undesired past event/experience will eventually show up again in their present or future regardless of what they do. However, that's not a very realistic train of thought.

Yesterday you may have had eggs and toast for breakfast and the day before you ate oatmeal, and the day before that you drank a super green smoothie. If past events (beneficial or not, important or insignificant) were destined to repeat no matter what you tried to do about it, then you would still be sipping warm breast or canned milk for breakfast, lunch *and* dinner!

Most of us know this type of outcome is not likely and would never happen to a thriving, healthy being. Things have a way of changing and they always will. Why am I so certain things will always change? That's an easy question to answer.

For better or worse, we have the ability to change our understanding, thoughts, feelings and desires thereby changing our reality. Whether it's apparent to us or not, at some point we each desire to ascend, to rise above, move beyond or simply add to a certain experience in some way.

We're either envisioning moving up to the next level or remaining at a current one. Moving up or staying put; whether it's a slow or fast, physical or mental process, we're always going somewhere be it desired or not desired.

We've all witnessed what happens when one continues to resist elevating themselves within any crucial area of life. Some form of atrophy, stagnation even death is eminent. They eventually get stale, stinky and pass on or get passed over! The collective keeps right on evolving whether an individual decides to stink or not!

Consider this, have you ever wondered why those little pint-sized replicas of us eventually give up the bottle? They are inspired by watching us eat! Not to mention being inundated by all the different consumable colors, shapes, textures and wonderful aromas floating around them.

Milk just doesn't cut it after a while as it is not enough to sustain a fast-growing baby. Hence the reason they get to a point where they're ravenously hungry (desiring more) *and* grumpy--impatient to have more now! They are preparing for an increase by cutting teeth. Now, who needs teeth to consume milk?

But even while going through growing pains, babies remain courageous! Those little pint-sized beings don't fear the unknown but embrace it. They do so without debating themselves to death and without knowing they're being courageous at all.

Babies are naturally open to allowing various channels (mama, dada, binky, etc.) to bring to them the things they enjoy. They have no knowledge of the dynamics associated with abundance or for what they need to thrive, but they are aware that feel good things (abundance) comes to them in many forms.

Maybe we should relearn how to be courageous like babies. If we were to relax and allow both known and unknown beneficial forces to assist us, it would facilitate a seamless interaction between those known or unknown forces and our own creative ones.

Can you then imagine the variables for a desired change occurring with all of that working in your favor? It would be astronomical! *But* until a person comes to a better understanding of the term "realistic," it will be difficult if not impossible to experience those deeply desired things that keep eluding them.

Your desires, feelings, words and thoughts all have to be in unison, on one accord. In spiritual terminology, this is what's known as being vibrationally aligned. And you must learn to keep yourself that way for longer than a nanosecond! Here's one more example of how we get out of alignment with the things we desire:

"I am never going to make this payment deadline! Why am I always late paying my bills?"

Can you see what was asked of the brain to focus on? In this question the brain has been commanded to work on, to pull up past experiences of **never** meeting payment deadlines, and to **not** make payments on time.

That's definitely the WRONG question to ask. It's a double negative whammy! Even your body gives you an obvious clue concerning the questions negativity. It tenses up! Your neck, traps, shoulders and stomach are in knots and your head gets so heavy, you result to the woe-is-me head rest within the palm of hand position! And no, that's not an energy freeing Yoga pose. Try asking these questions instead:

"How can I pay my bills on time? Why is it I'm so excited and

100

happy to pay them before they are even due?"

These are better questions to ask your brain to focus on and to find an example of, because always making your payments on time is the thing you'd rather do. Did you notice a sense of relief or ease when reading these questions as opposed to the previous ones? Again, this is the body giving you a clue.

Wording your question in this way is not being unrealistic, because I'm sure you have paid at least one bill on time before. Even if you haven't accomplished this feat yet, you've seen others do it. It is not an unknown concept for you to digest or to believe.

If it has been done before by anyone then it's possible for little ole you to do it as well! Forming your questions in this way makes it easier for you to become a full-fledged, honorary student of the *I Can Do It Too Institution of Higher Thought!* Get it? I sure hope so because this is how you change the way you think and feel.

If you do not change from the hurtful, negative ways you think and speak about yourself and others, you will not be able to change or move past those undesired manifestations you keep drawing into your experience. It will be almost impossible to acquire that which you truly desire.

It feels great when you know without a doubt that your cup (your reservoir of desires) is always full, and just moments away from tipping over and pouring its contents all over you! Right? However, on the flip side, when you constantly worry or fear that your cup is already tapped out and is empty with a gigantic hole in the bottom of it, that feels scary and horrible!

Knowing that abundance is at your command fosters faith, perseverance, excited anticipation and joy—all the things you'd prefer to experience. Doubting or flat out disbelieving you have the ability to manifest abundance in any form fosters hopelessness, resistance/struggle, fear and usually unworthiness or victimization—none of the things you want to experience at all.

The sooner you become and stay aware of the things coming out of you, those things being your thoughts, words and feelings, the easier it will be to manifest the things you really want. It's just that simple and that crucial.

Now that you know how to form the best questions (which is the first step when creating your personal MAP) you must learn how to follow up with the very best response/action to the inspiring answers you are expecting to receive.

Being happy and excited about your cup runneth over responses before you ever receive what you desire seems like putting the cart before the horse doesn't it? However, as a benefit to this seemingly backward arrangement, some answers will come in the form of your manifested desires! Now how mind blowing is that?

Remember, *you* are the script writer, director, lead and supporting actor plus the devoted fan of your life story. So, make it believably fantastic for you! Here's an example of a follow up response/action statement:

"Since I will be paying all my bills on time, I'm feeling much more empowered, as if I can do anything I set my heart and mind to accomplish. Now that I don't have late fees to contend with, I can find ways to save more money.

In no time at all I will have saved enough for that weekend trip to Montreal I've been thinking about. Not only will I be able to visit friends there, I can shop for special gifts to give to friends and family when I return. They'll get such a bang out of that! And who knows, I just might meet someone special while I'm there..."

I don't know about you, but just reading that stimulated those happy, empowering feelings in me! And you have to admit, it's a far cry from the woe is me story one could be telling themselves, and falling deeper into a state of depression or hopelessness because of it.

Write and envision your follow up story as if it's the wonderful life you desire to experience right now! Make it real, fun, bring it to life by giving it meaning and feeling. Add to it an air of excitement and before long, you will have incorporated this way of thinking and speaking into every area of your life! Everything will be possible and nothing will be insurmountable. Isn't *that* a MAP you'd love to rely on?

Now that you have these two steps, here's the third component. Read, listen to, recite (I prefer the word reenact over recite, and I'll explain why I do in just a bit) or contemplate on your MAP as many times a day as you feel led to. But **never ever** stress over the process.

Remember, emotional stress is fear in disguise and is what stalls your progress. Allow things to come about at a natural, stress-free pace. Go about living your life and enjoying it while you are anticipating your desires coming to fruition.

As a matter of fact, there will be times when you will not think about your MAP at all! Which can be just as productive because you are no longer worrying or stressing about if or when those desires will become a reality.

What this means is you have either abandoned your desires or you've come to know that it's only a matter of time until they become evident! And just in case you're wondering, you will not have to invest in a tally counter either.

There's no magic number of repetitions you must hold

yourself to performing. It all depends on what you need to hear, feel or think about that will get and keep you aware, connected to your intuitive gut, and on track with your anticipated experiences and desires.

Speaking of your anticipated desires, here is the perfect spot to interject my reasons for preferring one word over of another. Especially since the word relates to hearing, speaking and feeling your MAP at its highest potential!

I'm sure you're familiar with the word recite, which means to repeat aloud from memory; to state stats or facts in order. You also know the word re-enact, which means to act out, to perform a past or previous event. Now that we've covered English 101, let's delve into Manifesting 3.0!

For some who have not quite figured out the steps involved with manifesting, they may take on the practices of others. This is quite understandable because they're not sure how to successfully manifest the things they have been unable to thus far. But they most definitely want to be successful at it!

They have been told that reciting certain commands (or demands) for a specific number of times, facing one of the four cardinal directions, focusing on a particular object, or preforming certain body movements or poses will enable them to receive that which they desire. That is, if any or all of these steps are done correctly!

Done correctly or not, rituals devoid of any heart-felt emotional connection; of the belief that one is already worthy of and willing to prepare themselves for that which they are seeking, is the equivalent of uttering a bunch of pointless babble with a bit of unusual posturing thrown in!

No one is moved by that, not even the one performing the ritual! You've got to invest all of you in your manifestation process. In other words, you need to understand the significance of and be in complete agreement with the words you will speak, as well as any ritualistic procedure you will perform.

If not, you might as well be whistling a beautiful melody in gale force winds for all the good it will *not* do! But maybe this down-home, southern form of articulation will help get my point across to you:

"Not feeling and believing it? Not getting it!"

Your manifestation process is uniquely personal. Don't feel you must mimic the rituals of another unless it resonates with you and you're deeply invested. Neither should you measure yourself against someone else's accomplishments or regressions. You have no idea how much time or the degree of dedication they have given to their process.

Make this all about you and leave others out of the equation. Though some will try to convince you otherwise, no one can change, think or feel for you except you! If you are serious about changing to empower your life, then this is the point where you get to be very selfish and focus more on your personal wellbeing and unique growth process.

It's important for you to grow *in* before you can to grow up! Your growth and awareness process must be sustainable, real and enjoyable. If it's not, then doubts, fears, impatience or boredom will eventually creep up and derail your progress.

However, getting back on track after a derailment is doable. Actually, you do it all the time. When you stumble and fall down, eventually you get back up. But don't you feel it's much easier and less nerve racking to be proactive instead of reactive?

Remember, fear or stress will **never** attract the fearless, carefree experiences you desire to have. It cannot because fear, stress (or any emotion or thought) pulls along with it more of the same. You already know this to be true.

Once I've written my MAP and it resonates with me, I sometimes record myself saying it with enthusiasm and excitement. I have a couple of those recordings on my website. Stop by and check them out.

It's very easy to make a recording on your cell phone, an mp3 player or a computer, and then listen to it whenever the feeling hits you! You can even add music to your recorded MAP, but don't let the music overshadow your voice, because it's important to hear and feel *you* speaking those words of empowerment.

Also, if you listen to a recording of your MAP, speak along with it occasionally. There is a power (a vibrational resonance) that emanates from the words you speak. Your MAP is a motivational method designed by you, for you. Which is a much better option than listening to some stranger's voice who doesn't know your unique life experiences, but is telling you how and what you should think, feel and speak!

We all have common experiences, but where one person views an experience as interesting, another will feel that same experience to be boring. Because we perceive "common" experiences differently and have different levels of awareness and understanding, no single approach, method, belief or activity will work for everyone every time.

Question. Is anyone better able to express your experiences and desires than you? I'll answer that for you-- No! You can't get it more customized *and* personal than if you do this yourself!

When first starting out, I highly recommend re-enacting/remembering your MAP just before falling asleep or first thing in the morning, or both! Why do this before falling asleep and/or first thing in the morning?

Well, if you're like most, you may have several demands for your attention and focus during the day. And because we don't always do a good job of relaxing and letting those demands go, sometimes we need a way to avoid bringing them to bed with us. Nope, those demands of yours are *not* good bed partners!

Can you think of a better way to release anxieties and fears then by reenacting/remembering your highly anticipated desires and experiences? Doing so will give you a reprieve from those stressful demands you sometimes drag around with you during the day.

Actually, there's another raved about technique proven to help one release anxieties and fears, but requires assistance from a second (wink, wink...*very intimate*) party. These types of techniques have been described in many books for many years, so I need not go there in this one.

There's a huge benefit to having a technique you can implement at any time; one which doesn't require assistance from a second party *and* helps you drop most or all of your unproductive resistance and baggage quickly and easily.

Just imagine how much better it will be to simply allow pleasant reminders of what's coming your way to calm and revive you. You can feel at ease and even fall asleep while listening to and envisioning your very own personally tailored, coming soon, new and exciting reality!

The same technique can be applied upon awakening. Sometimes we wake up remembering the things we've left undone, or we'll have concerns of repeating a set of unfortunate events as Bill Murray did in the movie Groundhog Day.

I'm sure you know this is not the most empowering way to start your day. Again, you'll have to find a way to release these disempowering feelings even if it's just for a few minutes. Reenacting or remembering the next exciting adventure in your life will help you do just that!

However, if you're having one of those mornings or evenings in which you are heavily resistant to letting go of your concerns or worries, then you may have to reenact or play your recording a few times to realize some degree of relief.

Also, accepting how you feel can help when dealing with a pending Groundhog Day. Acknowledge and then accept the fact that it's okay to sometimes feel impatient, fearful or doubtful because you're still learning how to strengthen and pump up your gut (faith) muscles!

Give yourself a pat on the back for at least being aware of your unfounded fears. Remember, at one time those fears and doubts of yours rode you long and hard before you ever realized how awful your steadfast belief in them made you feel.

Try reminding yourself often of the reason you have decided to engage in this re-empowerment activity. Hopefully your reason, your why is much bigger and more desired than any fears, doubts or impatience that crops up.

Never forget that the life you are living is due to the choices you are making. Yes, the buck starts and stops with you! Best case scenario, you will lean on this understanding, that you are much stronger than you once perceived yourself to be and more open to all the wonderful potentials that will always await you.

Or you'll abandon the idea of living your desires and accept only what you can currently see, or have witnessed in the past. But know that your past is only the accumulation of experiences/events like the one you just experienced a moment ago. Wait for it…yes! You are now experiencing a moment that once was your future. Oh snap! That moment is now your past!

Get it? you were there in that moment, you experienced it and now it's entirely up to you to do something new, something different in this present moment. That is, if you desire something different in a future, present moment. That's exactly how Bill did it! Sounds complicated but it's not.

The shifts we make between past, present and future seem pretty Sci-Fi doesn't it? But within our current capabilities we always experience things in the present. When we remember past events or envision future ones, we do so in this present moment.

However, when we repeatedly reenact past thoughts and experiences, it is equivalent to living a perpetual Groundhog Day. This is an existence in which one fails to take advantage of hindsight, or to understand that there are moments in life that need to be acted upon differently *if* change is desired.

The same goes for lingering in thoughts of any desired future experiences. You may know this as pie in the sky thinking or daydreaming. Excessive daydreaming of the future while ignoring present life experiences and lessons will more than likely keep one in a state of uninspired inaction.

It will be hard if not impossible for one to advance towards a desired future when they are so unaware, and take so little inspired action while they are existing in the present moment! If you desire change, then you will have to do some things differently.

Keep what works, drop with does not and know that you can always initiate something new, fresh and inspirational at any time. But if during any perceived groundhog moments additional infusions of empowerment is needed, I recommend bringing along headphones to get your empowerment party started!

In essence, what you will be doing is similar to fine tuning and maintaining your automobile, especially the engine control unit. This is the brains of your ride and its purpose is to regulate many, actually all of its critical functions.

I'm believing you'd love to enjoy most if not all of the unique and interesting road trips life has in store for you. If this is the case, then it's important that you at least prepare in advance to increase the odds that you will! Keeping your vehicle (self) in optimal condition, being prepared for any contingencies (which is much easily then you think) and having an accurate road map is essential.

That is, if you intend to experience safe, exciting and beneficial excursions or extended trips. What are some probable consequences if you don't take care of and prepare yourself?

Well, due to long-term neglect you'll have to contend with costly physical and emotional repairs or adjustments. You will also have to take responsibility for being the main contributor of your unpleasant circumstances, which you may have easily avoided or lessened to some degree had you been more proactive.

And finally, having to deal with feelings of frustration or hopelessness as you wander in circles---lost because you've relied on an old, out-of-date, disempowering, past experiences map.

Neither of the consequences I mentioned will get you to that desired place unscathed! Not when you've set yourself up to have several minor or major breakdowns while in route. Just imagine the following:

You veer too far off your chosen path and end up in a place aptly named Lostville. Not only are you lost, but some vital part of your vehicle is no longer working as it should, and you have no idea what's broken or how to fix it.

What if there's no one knowledgeable enough to help with repairs, you have no signal and no power left in your communication device, and no one comes along to inquire if you need help? Right off the bat, you know it will not be the great road trip you desired.

After days, months or years of maintenance neglect, the unavoidable has happened. The only choice you have left is to pop open the hood, look inside and see if you can figure something out. What do you think you'll find once you take a look under that hot, smoking mess?

You're likely to have no idea, but you do sense that what you'll find will not make you happy. Sure enough, most of your vital energizing fluids have leaked out, and your creative spark plugs are covered in old, burnt, debilitating sludge. How encouraging is that?

Since you are now forced to take a closer look at your circumstances, you can't help but to notice you've been rolling on low-to-no inspirational support while treading haphazardly!

What about that uncomfortable wobble and tremor you sometimes experience when turning a sharp corner, backing up, slowly creeping forward or quickly accelerating? Yes, your frontend is bent and is causing you to tilt dangerously to the left. You are very much out of alignment!

To add to your dismay, you are now operating within the confines of Murphy's Law. Things tend to get worse *before* they get better. What you once thought was a little harmless dirt turns out to be shavings from your automatic braking system.   Yep! Your ability to safely stop before things get too far out of control has been compromised as well!

Now I ask you, do you really want to take a trip--short or extended, without making sure you've done all that you can to enjoy a safe and comfortable round trip, and that you won't get or stay lost for very long?

Do you want to be successful at navigating towards the experiences you desire?   Yes?   Then it would be wise to prepare yourself and get familiar with a MAP. If not, you will eventually end up lost within a maze of contradictory experiences and unsure of how to get to your chosen destination from there!

CHAPTER 9

GIVE ME FIVE GRUNT!

Grunt is a military term used when referring to an infantry member of the Marine Corps and Army. Grunts receive much tougher training because they do the heavy gunning. They are the ones called to walk right into the heat of direct combat, to do some serious butt kicking!

I'm guessing that right about now you're a little leery and wondering how the military term grunt relates to you. Not to worry, you are by no means in the Army now, and hopefully you're no longer at war with yourself or anyone else for that matter. The only weapon you will need to pack and load is that of your favorite pocket notebook or recorder, mp3 player, Android or iOS device. And whereas there is a slight learning curve, (the construction of and being consistent with your MAP) training is not that difficult to complete.

However, you will be called upon to kick some serious buts, no getting around that one. It's the reason you're here right? I'm guessing you'd love to eliminate any threats from all enemy buts So, from this day forward, you will exercise your power to eradicate all threats to your total prosperity by implementing the five recon missions listed below. Pay close attention grunt!

Refrain/Reform: Refrain, stop yourself from using disempowering, negative thoughts and speech. Reform by changing both your internal and external talk.

Reconstruct: Reconstruct to better enhance your brain's problem solving abilities by forming the best questions *and* actions (your follow up story) for it to access. These Q&A's will be used to construct your MAP.

Recognize & Release: Any fears, all **F**alse **E**xpectations **A**ppearing **R**eliable are to be annihilated with impunity. Do not play around with them, do not entertain them--debunk them! **Note:** This is where you *must* kick some serious buts.

Recall & Reinforce: Recall and reinforce your **MAP.** Recall those experience or things you intend to do, have or be. Remember how wonderful it feels just thinking about them and knowing they're coming your way! If reinforcement is required, then listen to an audio recording of your MAP as many times as needed, but especially first thing in the morning or the last thing you do before falling asleep. This will help to reinforce your new, uplifting, fearless, *"I can!"* mindset.

Repeat: Repeat as often as needed and for as long as you desire. It can take longer than 30 days to change an undesired, long standing habit, so stick with it if this relates to you. Better yet, see this process as gaining a habit you *do* desire to have for the long term! If you look at it in this way, you're not losing much but gaining a lot!

Also, steps one, two and three should be acted upon immediately; whenever fear and harmful thoughts and talk crops up. You will repeat these steps when creating a new MAP or when modifying a current one.

Note: Fears are usually hidden beneath other emotions we don't normally associate as fear. Depression, anxiety, worry or shame are just a few of the fear-based emotions we often experience. Fear takes on many forms and will hinder you if you are not aware of its presence and influence. I have more information about fears on my website and I think you'll be surprised to learn what fear is not.

Well, now you have it. The only thing left for you to do is to put your MAP to the test. Keep your mind open and aware, take note of everything that happens after you begin using your mapping process, but by all means use it!

When you begin navigating from your MAP, you will find that some things will materialize very quickly, within the hour or the day. Others will take a bit longer, but that's fine because more than likely you'll have plenty of quickies!

One unexpected quickie that totally blew me away, occurred around the exact time I was in the initial phases of formulating ideas for this book and a few others. It happened in December of 2014.

The venue was our annual Christmas party, a party I almost opted out of attending. I was very excited about the ideas I had for this book in particular. Spending as much time as possible working on those ideas seemed more appealing to me than attending a party.

But for some odd reason I started remembering all the great prizes given away at the end of these company sponsored parties. As soon as the thought of those great prizes popped into my head, I made a MAP on the fly. I didn't write it down but spoke it. It went a little something like this:

"I'm going to this Christmas party because I'm winning some money tonight!"

Yeah, sounds a bit superficial, right? Hey, happens to the best of us. To make a long story short, that evening I and two coworkers left work to attend the party. However, this time I participated in a few games in order to win tickets for the drawings of those wonderful prizes.

Initially, there were four of us seated at the table with two more seats in reserve for another co-worker and her guest. The last two members of our group were running a bit late, but eventually they arrived and all intended attendees were grouped together. I've given you our seating arrangement for a reason.

Finally, after playing games and winning chips for tickets, after all the speeches and announcements were concluded, the time we'd all been waiting for had come. Prize time! But before any prize winners were called, I made another bold declaration, this time in front of witnesses:

"Everyone in our group will win something tonight!"

At the time, I had no idea what possessed me to say such a thing, and I think I know what you're thinking possessed me. I'll just state for the record that no, I wasn't inebriated; not even tipsy.

Regardless of the reason, shortly after my impromptu announcement, the prize presenter called the first two winning tickets. The fact that neither of the winners were anywhere near our table didn't even faze me.

They were only the first two winners of many more to come. So why should I panic? But would you care to guess who the third winner was? You've got it! I was the happy winner of a $50 gift certificate and before the night was over, we would be the top winning table!

Here's the breakdown of our winnings. The two coworkers I arrived at the event with also won gift certificates. Another coworker won a nice home accessory prize and her assistant won one of those fancy digital toaster ovens.

The boyfriend of the assistant did not play to win tickets for the drawings *but* won the last prize of the night–a winning Lotto scratch off ticket that had been hidden within our table's centerpiece decoration. Go figure!

Of course, there were several other winners at the party that night, but no table had all winners sitting at it *except* ours. Now you can call what happened to all of us at that table coincidence or luck if doing so makes you feel more comfortable.

As for me, I was already sold on this process before the night of that Christmas party. Things were already happening in my life that could not be chalked up to mere coincidence or luck—not that I believe in such craziness as coincidence or luck anyway!

For most of my life I've sensed that there was more to living than meets the eye. Thankfully this feeling is not unique to me, but unfortunately many of us get far too busy navigating around life to even recognize it.

Nevertheless, the sense of something else to life remains. It even reveals itself every now and again. Just beyond the outskirts, in that peripheral field where one's ability to physically see is either greatly diminished or completely obscured, exists an intelligent and powerful conduit.

It's a creative energy which works quietly, effortlessly. Until a few years ago, I wondered about all the obscurity related to this unseen source of conscious energy. I don't wonder about it anymore. For me, the concept of it seems similar to the layperson's understanding of air. We can feel it but can't see it, and most of us don't have a clue as to how air even exist.

As very young children we had no concept of air at all. Someone had to enlighten us; give us a name to reference it by, explain what we were feeling and why it was essential that we did. Now, as enlightened beings in the know, the concept of air is a given—a known mystery.

We've come to accept the fact that air *is* because it is felt/sensed. It is a force, a space that can be manipulated by inhaling and exhaling, fanning it across our skin or navigating various air crafts through it!

We can't see it or hold in our hands, but we can see and feel how it inner acts and affects our physical bodies *and* everything around us. Is that not magic? Are you beginning to wonder if we have another sensory organ to rely on?

Yes, the eyes, ears, nose, skin and tongue will always be extremely useful bio tools to have. However, without some type of cutting edge, innovative technology to assist the severely impaired, it would be impossible for them to independently navigate safely and successfully in this world without the use of at least two of those bio tools. And of the two, one has to be either sight or sound.

But have you ever stopped to consider why most of us who are very proficient with utilizing all five bio senses, tend to be less than successful in certain areas of life? Especially if we are to believe that aside from a little common sense, the most essential tool needed to assist us in life is that of the brain's ability to correctly interpret the things we see, hear, smell, touch or taste.

However, when interpreting what the brain has relayed

through our five senses, the application of a little common or logical sense sometimes falls extremely shy of enlightening us as to all there is to know. In other words, there's usually more than meets the eyes, ears, nose, skin and tongue's interpretation.

Let's say you encounter what *appears* to be an upstanding, polite and helpful young man. He seems genuine and seems to do everything in a conscientious manner. His credentials are impeccable and everyone you've spoken to about him has nothing but good things to report.

However, your gut (and every cell in your body) warns you that he is neither and is not to be trusted. You take heed to that warning, and only a few days later you find out your intuitive gut was correct.

Let's apply what your ears may hear, but is better amplified through that "other" sensory organ. Someone known or unknown to you speaks calmly, eloquently and with knowledge and conviction concerning a subject of interest.

Their demeanor remains posed and undisturbed throughout the oration. In theory, what they are saying is factual, but there's something about how they're saying it that doesn't feel right to you.

You somehow know they're lying about something, so you decide to trust your gut and not go along with whatever they're promoting. Later it is confirmed. They were lying like a rug! How is it some will tune in and recognize these signals while others will sense nothing, and fall for the falsity that presents itself as truth?

Could it be what many of us is failing to do is acknowledging, understanding and putting to better use this other sensory organ? An organ that feels as if it originates from the core/gut of our physical bodies but radiates far beyond it. It appears capable of vastly outperforming the brain, is a connective link between each of us *and* a very powerful, knowledgeable yet noninvasive force.

In other words, it's extremely helpful if you rely on it, but will not nag you to death if you don't. Also, has our total dependency on organs that are extremely helpful but limited in some ways, been instrumental in helping to conceal this deeply misunderstood component of our existence?

This is by no means some none essential component of human existence, but is a key element which seems essential for our continued success and expansion. I don't believe we'd exist or that our existence would be the same without it. One would think that with so many hurting, disillusioned and disenfranchised people in the world, we would want to know as much as possible concerning this thing that has been felt or sensed by every being on the planet, at least one time or another.

Again, religion, philosophy and science have each had their say about this matter, but for the most part their input has resulted in many feelings divided, fearful and intolerant.

I think these questions will only be resolved through each individual's quest for the answers. Apparently, no one individual or organization can provide unbiased, adequate answers *or* questions for the whole, for all of us.

We are each responsible for asking these individual questions, and through higher awareness we can better respond to those higher, more enlightened answers we will receive. In this way the many truly becomes the one.

Does one tap into this source or do we simply allow it to flow within us? Can we turn it up or down? Is it essential for enriching one's day-to-day life? Are we able to connect with it as many times as we like, or can we stay connected for life? Exactly how does one do that?

Those were just a few of the questions I asked concerning this intuitive organ we seem to possess *and* to utilize, but without knowing very much about how the process works.

Throughout the ages and from every corner of the globe, wise men and women, saints and sages, master teachers, shaman and other highly enlightened individuals have walked this earth for what appears to be one reason only. It seems they had an urgent desire to bestow upon us a very powerful message. They were deeply driven to share, teach and enlighten us of that which appeared to have been hidden from us, but was actually in plain sight!

For those with sight, those with an ear to listen, their messages become much clearer. We were instructed to first seek the benevolent force inside of us. It is this inner force which holds the key to unlocking, liberating, changing and affecting not only the inner person, but all the outer stuff of life one desires to experience as well. Now that you know what I have learned, make use of it. Play around with it, tweak it, make it your own so that it works best for you.

But please, don't ever think you will not be challenged again in life because you now have access to the Inner Creator's technique! Thinking in that way would be a mistake. Never forget that hidden within every challenge you face is a gentle (or in some cases not so gentle) nudge designed to get you out of your lazy boy/girl comfort zone. They are meant to empower and not to destroy you.

Actually, challenges come about because you've asked for them via some type of increase you desire to experience. Be it a better job, a loving co-creative partnership, being debt free, owning your own home or your very own plot of Green Acres! However, you cannot receive any of these things if you are not willing to release the other things you no longer desire to experience, but have become accustomed to sticking with.

Let's say your current job is one in which you no longer enjoy because there's nothing more you can bring to it, and it can't take you any further. Does it still feel like the best job for you, or is it you're just afraid to go for that job or business you truly desire? What about the unequal partnership in which you are both equally dissatisfied, and completely unwilling to work on it together? How much of a loving feeling and co-creative satisfaction is either of you experiencing in *that* relationship?

And how are you expecting to ever be debt free or own a home when you continue to rack up more debt, over spend and not save one copper penny? Does uncontrollable spending and debt collection drama feel like you're anywhere near the road to financial freedom?

Complacency, bullheadedness, compulsive or addictive habits are challenging, but they are not deal breakers. They can be used to help you check in, to realign, to become stronger, more centered and to then adjust any imbalance in your life.

Challenges can wake you up to the possibilities of recreating, experiencing and expressing a better you! But you have to be willing to allow change to occur by letting go of some stuff. Stuff like harmful or unbeneficial thinking, talking and actions.

Real change will not happen until you do. If you're willing to recognize the enlightened lesson a challenge provides and take inspired action, then you are actually preparing yourself to receive, to allow that which you desire to experience.

Doesn't that beat the heck out of you feeling oppressed or trapped in a situation you didn't enjoy experiencing even *before* the challenge came along? Think of it this way, you'd be bored silly if you didn't have new challenges to inspire your unlimited creativity, awareness and understanding. So, count it all good!

Well here we are, at your new chapter beginning! Now

the only thing left for you to do is to put your shiny new wheels on the road and test drive that puppy! Up for a road trip? Yeah…I think you are.

Yvonne L. Jones

AFTERWORD

I'm so thrilled you made it this far, and it's my desire that you resonate with some, best case scenario *most* of the things in this book. It was truly written with you in mind. Anything I stumble across that helps to uplift, inspire and positively affect another human being is well worth the effort in my book. Pun most definitely intended!

As a matter of fact, it is my pleasure to share the things I have sought out, labored over and then put to good use. Sharing good news is more than a pleasure as I seem unable to stop myself. I truly believe that no one is alone in their seeking of answers, in their desire to co-create with others or when navigating through any life lessons presented to them.

There is always that ripple effect in which we are each touched by and become beneficiaries of it—the life lesson. Whether the ripple is unsettling and over whelming, or gentle and buoyant, we can grow with either!

By the way, if you're interested in streamlining your search for more inspirational, thought provoking, life enhancing material, I'd like to share access to a lot of great free stuff (audios, books, websites, blogs and videos) that were extremely helpful during my learning and transformational process.

Now, don't let some of the books or website titles frighten you. For example, one author easily explains the correlation between manifesting your desires and quantum physics. He really does! It's not difficult to comprehend either.

As a matter of fact, it should lead you to a greater

understanding of yourself, of the universe and your place in it. You'll find all of this great stuff and more at Little Sepia Books, my publishing website.

Okay, here's something I'd love for you to do. Please accept my invitation to become a VIP subscriber! It's no hassle and also free. Just what does a VIP subscriber receive you ask?

Once a month you'll receive one or any of the following; new blog posts, chapter excerpts of upcoming books, new book release updates, a chance to participate in book promotions, giveaways, contests and other great stuff.

Here's what you will *not* receive as a VIP subscriber-- more than one email/newsletter per month from me. How can I make such a bold promise while committing a fairly uncommon marketing no-no?

Easy, I'm a writer and I spend a big chunk of my energy crafting new and interesting material I can't wait to share with you. What that means is this, I'm neither motivated or remotely interested in inundating your inbox with emails. You can stop jumping for joy now.

Well, it appears we've come to the end of this book. But before you go, I'd like to thank you for allowing me to share my thoughts and experiences. You could have found several exciting things to do, none of which included being with yours truly *but* you chose to spend this time with me. I so appreciate that!

Also, I hope you were able to digest most or all of my gut enriching discoveries and techniques, and that you were able to laugh a little and have some fun as well. Until next time.

Enjoy!

ABOUT THE AUTHOR

Yvonne L. Jones is a native of Houston, Texas. She is an Inspirational Life Ambassador in training and the author of another insightful how-to book, *How To Feel In Love And Not Fall For The Wrong One In 60 Seconds Or Less,* as well as two books of poetry, *At the River's Edge Where Quantum Streams Flow* and *Speaking Out and Listening In.*

For information about the author, new books and audio release dates, the benefits of becoming a VIP reader and to grab your **free** relationship e-book, visit:
https://lsbpublishing.com/contact

If you have enjoyed this Little Sepia Book, please take just a moment and give it an honest review at:
https://amazon.com/author/yvonne

Thank You!

.

www.ingramcontent.com/pod-product-compliance
Lightning Source LLC
Chambersburg PA
CBHW061733020426
42331CB00006B/1227